$f$P

# IT'S ALL ABOUT YOU

## *Live the Life You Crave*

Mary Goulet
and Heather Reider

FREE PRESS

NEW YORK   LONDON   TORONTO   SYDNEY

FREE PRESS
A Division of Simon & Schuster, Inc.
1230 Avenue of the Americas
New York, NY 10020

First Free Press hardcover edition September 2007

FREE PRESS and colophon are trademarks of Simon & Schuster, Inc.

For information about special discounts for bulk purchases,
please contact Simon & Schuster Special Sales at 1-800-456-6798
or business@simonandschuster.com

Designed by Julie Schroeder

Manufactured in the United States of America

10   9   8   7   6   5   4   3   2   1

Library of Congress Cataloging-in-Publication Data

Goulet, Mary
It's all about you: live the life you crave / Mary Goulet and Heather Reider.
—1st Free Press hardcover ed.
p. cm.
1. Mothers—Psychology. 2. Mothers—Conduct of life. 3. Self-realization in
women. I. Reider, Heather, II. Title.
HQ759.G6297 2007
306.874'3—dc22            2007004373

ISBN-13: 978-1-4165-4509-5
ISBN-10:     1-4165-4509-3

*To our children:*
*Sterling, Portia, Evan, Hayden, and Nolan.*

*They are our daily inspiration.*

# CONTENTS

# IT'S ALL ABOUT YOU

*Chapter 1*

# In Search of the Unique You

It's a wonderful feeling to know you're unique, that you have unique ideas, a unique look, a unique family, and a unique perspective on the world. It's an amazing gift that we give when we add our unique twist to any situation. On a grand scale, it's knowing that you make a difference, that who you are is important to your kids, family, friends, community, and the world at large.

Let's start with the title of this book, *It's All About You*. We gave the book this title because taking care of you is important, because you take care of everyone else. We struggled with this title because we know women often feel guilty focusing time and attention on themselves. We know this because we struggle with the feeling as well. We think when we take time for ourselves, we're taking time away from our families. And no one wants to do that. In truth, when we take time to do something good for ourselves, everyone around us benefits. It all starts with you.

Think about what's going on in the world today—famine, war,

single moms living in poverty, and a divorce rate that is through the roof. All of those things tear at your soul. In order for you to make a difference, you have to feel good about your life. It might seem like a stretch that getting organized might help the famine in Africa, but getting organized with your finances might free up $20 to write a check, and getting your schedule organized might free up time to volunteer. Along the same line, when you organize your closet, you may find a warm coat to donate. It's the little gestures in life that have a big impact. You must believe you make a difference.

---

Be the change you want to see in the world.

—*Mahatma Gandhi*

---

We are Mary and Heather, hosts of our own talk radio show, founders of MomsTown.com, and publishers of MomsTown Magazine. We are both wives and mothers. Mary stays busy with two girls, and Heather keeps on the move with three boys. Three years ago we met online and discovered we lived in the same zip code. Fate? We think so. At the time, each of us had a struggling home-based business and we were going into debt faster than we were making a profit. After a brief phone call, we decided to meet for coffee, and before we'd finished sipping the steamed milk off our lattes, we knew—the connection between us was unique. We were both moms who wanted to lead vibrant, purposeful lives. We wanted to be good moms and wives and to build fantastic careers. And we knew we weren't alone. We had sisters and loads of girlfriends with the same craving—women who wanted to do exciting things and create possibilities. You will find in these pages the inspiration, motivation, and practical tips and resources to help you discover—or, in many cases, *rediscover*—the creative, independent, vibrant, and confident you.

We are in the fortunate position of communicating with lots of women every day. In fact, the theme that we have the power to create opportunity came from one of our radio listeners. She sent us an e-mail asking us, "How did you get the fantastic job of hosting Moms-Town Radio?"

We responded, "We made it up." At first the question struck us as funny, because apparently our listener thought MomsTown was some big conglomerate and we were hired by some suit and received a weekly paycheck. Truth is, Mary hired Heather and Heather hired Mary.

**We created our own opportunity—and you can too.**

Are we geniuses? Not really. (But don't tell our kids!) We're two women talking about the big issues that most women—and moms in particular—deal with every day. Like most women (and unlike most men), we've had to reinvent ourselves to be able to juggle marriage, motherhood, and moneymaking. In our past lives, Heather had a decade-long career as an on-air television reporter, and Mary was a Wall Street bond salesperson, a professional singer, and a licensed holistic health practitioner. Our own ideas and experiences were just a springboard for MomsTown.

---

Nobody is as smart as everybody.
— *William Taylor and Polly LaBarre*
*in* Mavericks at Work

---

Bright women are out there at the other end of the Internet, women like you. These are the women we hear from every day who are transforming themselves as businesswomen, artists, students, entrepreneurs. They are getting their lives back into balance, creating fulfilling lives, and offering their suggestions for helping others. And that's exactly what we were hoping might happen in our forum for women.

When we started MomsTown, our offices were in one of our guest rooms, and our husbands thought we were just dabbling in a hobby. Our computers were stationed on the bed and a phone cord stretched across the floor. We had to keep the window open (even when it was raining), because we were bootlegging the Internet connection from the downstairs home computer.

Now, thanks to a business that includes a radio show, website, and magazine, we've gone legit. You might even say we've arrived. We'd say we have a lot more possibility.

We decided to join forces, and we have ended up with more than double the creativity, energy, and success either of us had alone. Too often, women are afraid to ask for help, afraid to admit that they can't do it all by themselves. We overcame that fear, and so can you. In many of the upcoming chapters you'll find a recurring theme: decide what you want and be bold about asking for it. By believing in possibilities, you create opportunities.

For example, when we decided to merge our two businesses, we knew if we were going to crash and burn, we might as well do it together, Thelma & Louise style.

Three years later, we haven't crashed. We haven't burned. (Okay, maybe there was a time or two when we got a little scorched.) We're still working to help moms carve out a little extra income, a little extra time, a little extra energy, a little extra joy. It's rewarding work, and we're having a great time doing it.

None of this exempts us from the Monday-through-Friday morning looniness that is getting children out the door for school. We still spend our first waking hours wrestling children out of their beds and into their school clothes, making PB&Js, and carpooling. After that it's running errands, prepping dinner, and, oh yeah, working while the kids are busy at school learning and having fun. Then we pick them up, chauffeur them where they need to go, and never stop moving until our heads hit the pillows.

\* \* \*

This book is full of the issues we busy moms face every day that either create or stand in the way of our potential. We've taken topics from our show and from e-mails we've received from women around the world. We've put in our two cents, and we've included interviews with experts we consider the best in their fields.

> I'm a woman. I'm a mom. I want my own identity. I want to spend time with my friends. I want to feel in love. I'm worried about getting older. I could use more sleep. I would love to work out more. Perhaps I could take up a sport or a hobby, but when? I'm always short on time, short on energy, and I wonder every day what I will make for dinner. —Everymom

We're all trying to keep up, and too often we feel as though we're the only ones being left behind while everyone else is getting it all. Each of us is searching for the secret of how to achieve balance between work and home and how to find something that defines us.

**Life is like a conveyor belt of chocolates.**

Remember the I Love Lucy episode in which Lucy and Ethel were working in a chocolate factory? Apparently, even back in 1952, these two moms decided they needed to do more than just keep house. Their job was to pack chocolates in boxes, but the conveyor belt was moving so fast that they couldn't keep up. The result is something everyone should see. We'll never forget the image of them stuffing chocolates into their mouths, down their shirts, and in their apron pockets, all the while chocolates flying everywhere.

Moms often feel overwhelmed by the speed of their own conveyor belts. To avoid a meltdown, sometimes they have to slow the belt down, and sometimes they have to let a few chocolates get past them and fall to the ground. That's okay. We stress out when we think that we have to grab every morsel in life. But the truth is that life will keep delivering the sweet stuff to us. There also will be bittersweets along the way, but this book gives you strategies to maximize the happy moments. We're here to help you catch your breath and start living a life that's rich to you.

---

Because I am a woman, I must make unusual efforts to succeed. If I fail, no one will say, "She doesn't have what it takes." They will say, "Women don't have what it takes."

—*Clare Boothe Luce*

---

# TIPS AND TAKES FROM MOMSTOWN

Every day our inboxes are filled with e-mails from women around the world. They are active in our online community and anxious to share with one another. Women from all over America are quoted in this book. We will share with you their Tips and Takes. Regularly, we receive fresh and practical Tips about overcoming fears, making money from home, losing the last ten pounds, looking and feeling younger, getting organized, and making dinner.

We'll also share with you their Takes on issues we all face—how to handle a lagging libido (it's amazing how many of us would rather sleep than have sex), how to stand up to an educational system that seems to be sapping our kids of their creativity, and how to find more time in the day to do the things we love to do.

The outpouring from our community has been overwhelming. The women at MomsTown are working moms and stay-at-home moms.

They are happily married moms and single moms, and moms in troubled marriages. They are articulate, funny, and ambitious. Each woman is unique and has her own Take on the twenty-first-century issues with which we're dealing. Our community is open to all; the only thing we ask is that women check the Chick Factor at the log-in. Our community is about supporting one another, helping each other, and you're invited. We believe that as you read the chapters of this book, you will say, "That's me." Or "That's my girlfriend, or sister, or mom!"

## THE TOWN SITES

At that first coffee when we met and in the meetings that followed, it was clear that we wanted to create a community for women everywhere. We wanted women to have a place to pool knowledge and resources, to share stories and secrets. We knew that women wanted to connect virtually and meet locally. We are giving them the platform to do both. MomsTown is a welcoming place, where women can come for encouragement and practical advice—both giving and getting. In addition to our very active message board, we have hundreds of local MomsTown chapters, which we call Town Sites. There are Town Sites in every state, every province of Canada, in Europe and Australia, and the numbers continue to grow every day. The Town Sites are vital because they're local and grassroots. They are women getting together over coffee, just the way we did three years ago, to share possibilities and to share dreams. This puts us on the frontlines of the campaign for reclaiming and reinventing women's lives—and we're delighted to be here.

One gal Down Under called in to our show. She lives in a town with a population of sixty (yes, ten more than fifty, which probably qualifies it as a village rather than a town). She said she just had to call to say how relieved she was that there were other women out there who felt the way she did about wanting to be a fabulous mother, but also wanting to be more than a mother and fabulous at other stuff too.

## IS MONEY AN ISSUE?

One topic that arises regularly in the MomsTown discussions is money. Money is a major issue in women's lives. It affects how we live day in and day out. It affects our relationships and it affects our self-worth. Many of us moms started out in the working world; we held down a job and took home a paycheck, money we had earned. Whether it was big-n-fat or puny, it was our own. We were paid for work completed— a simple thing, really, but to us it was validating. Then we got married and became moms, and all of a sudden, we found ourselves in un-familiar economic terrain—financial terra incognita.

> *Women's battle for financial equality has barely been joined, much less won. Society still traditionally assigns to woman the role of money-handler rather than moneymaker, and our assigned specialty is far more likely to be home economics than financial economics.* —Paula Nelson

We found dividing our time between home and career exhausting. To spend more waking hours with our children, many of us segued into different jobs or careers, most likely with a smaller salary and a more flexible schedule. (Realistically, how many women do you know who happily took on *more* job responsibility, working *longer* hours, as a new parent?)

Or maybe we took a hiatus from the workforce entirely to become stay-at-home moms, at least at the start. Both of us did that, and we found that there's nothing that can bruise an ego like going from being a got-my-own-money kind of woman to feeling obliged to ask your husband for dough. Financial terra incognita started looking a lot like the Land of Begging, and we didn't like the scenery. With financial dependency on our husbands' incomes, money became an awkward, unpleasant topic and a source of tension and contention at home.

---

Remember, Ginger Rogers did everything Fred
Astaire did, but backwards and in high heels.

—*Bob Thaves*

---

We discovered that many other women were having the same experience. Maybe you got defensive about spending money on yourself, money you had not "earned." Or maybe you didn't spend it at all. If you ever felt guilty about "splurging" on yourself, we're playing your song.

What happened here? With our very understandable choice to work less outside the house in order to be available to our children, the balance of economic power between us and our spouses and between us and the outside world tilted. It's a problem the world over. Some husbands dole out money according to what *they* think you *ought* to need. Or perhaps you're still working a full-time job outside the home and you share your paycheck but he's not sharing the load. Either way, finances are a sticky issue in households, and we're about to shed new light on the age-old money fight.

**We call the money issues that come with marriage and motherhood the Money Shadow.**

That Money Shadow is the dark cloud that money can cast over a marriage. Lurking in that shadow are some biggies. We'll help you to nail 'em down and bring these taboo topics out of the closet. We're excited to share with our readers how Man Math and Lady Luck (the different ways men and women think and feel about money) play a prominent role in a woman's financial life. It's the kind of revelation that makes women breathe a huge sigh of relief: suddenly it all makes sense. We'll give you three money strategies that will change the way you think and talk (which is great for us, since we so often talk without thinking) about money, and your relationships around money.

These revelations have helped us and our community of women to put more cash in the bank and to defuse a volatile issue at home.

Why do we want to share our secrets with women the world over? Because we're all in this together. An inherent truth is that we need each other. Women need girlfriends, mothers, sisters, cousins, and aunts. It's been our experience that women need each other so much, they'll even reach out online trying to find someone who understands their wants, needs, hopes, and dreams.

## WHAT ABOUT SEX?

I know nothing about sex because I was always married.

—*Zsa Zsa Gabor*

Another truth is that motherhood often sends both energy and libido into a major free fall. We've got Tips to help readers deal with both. We're not afraid to admit there are times we'd rather sleep than have sex, but if we did that every night, we'd be well rested but single. When we were at a meeting talking about how to get an energy boost, Heather mentioned Red Bull. Someone said, "That stuff isn't good for you." Heather joked, "I know. I only drink it at night! It keeps my husband happy." Hmm, that's a great slogan: *Red Bull: Saving the Sex Lives of Married Couples.* But sex should be more than something that keeps your husband happy: it should make *you* happy too. You can make your own recipe from the best strategies we've come up with ourselves, and the gems that other women have contributed. Trust us—there are some real red-hot mamas out there.

# WHAT ABOUT FOOD?

We share emotional stories about how moms in the same boat have figured out some quick, easy ways to boost the health factor of the foods their families eat and have triumphed over the fatty stuff—without fad diet pills and plans. Don't take us wrong: this is not a diet book; we don't even include a diet chapter. It is a wake-up call that gets us all to start thinking about how we're feeding ourselves and our families.

We can't talk about bodies without talking about food. Food is another big issue for us moms who inherit a chef's hat (or a BlackBerry full of takeout phone numbers) once we have kids. Suddenly you go from nights out dining on foie gras (okay, maybe not foie gras, but at least grown-up food), to digging into bowl after bowl of mac 'n cheese made with fluorescent orange powder. Suddenly it's normal for us to eat snacks that come out of little plastic baggies. All this, um, stuff can take a toll on our bodies and our moods, but often these quick fixes are all we have time to give our kids and ourselves.

Body image is also something we all struggle with. Mention trying on bathing suits in any gathering of women, and you've got an instant support group. Girlfriends laugh with us in the best of times and hold us up through the worst of times. All too frequently, though, we let friendships wither because we are too busy with our day-to-day insanity. Friends need—and deserve—our attention, but we tend to give friendships a lower priority than our family. This is a mistake: when things fall apart, friends are what keep you going. It is important to explore the issues of friendship among women—how to reach out to make a friend if you feel isolated, how to sustain a friendship, and what to do with those high-maintenance pals who always need help but are never there when you need them.

# QUICKIES

Here's the reality: we know, no matter what it is you're doing right now or what you have on your to-do list, you don't have much time. So, throughout this book you'll find Quickies. Quickies are those moments when we skip the foreplay and the flowery talk and we just get it done. Quickies make you feel great, and they relieve stress in little time and with little effort.

A Quickie is manageable. It's a small chunk of time that we can all find in a day. Even if that means getting up fifteen minutes earlier than normal or staying up fifteen minutes later. Or maybe you can do a Quickie in those fifteen minutes between appointments, those fifteen minutes between dropping one son at swimming and picking the other up at soccer. Wherever you are, you can have a Quickie: at home, in the car, at the office.

We are living proof that anyone can live a better life with a few tiny tweaks. We're not saying, "Look at us, we do it all." In fact, it's exactly the opposite. You'll discover in this book that no one can do it all and that's okay! But that doesn't mean you can't have it all. To listen to people who tell us we can't have something is to cut our dreams off at the knees. If we believe we can't have something, we won't have it. It's as simple as that. We at MomsTown refuse to listen to the kind of chatter that whittles away at our aspirations, and we hope you will too.

**We need more moms dreaming about a better world if we want to live in a better world.**

Sure, there are realities that we must face. That's why we're turning to each other to get help with the obstacles that hold us back. We know this to be true: when moms unite, we are a force to be reckoned with.

Without leaps of imagination, or dreaming, we
lose the excitement of possibilities. Dreaming,
after all, is a form of planning.

—*Gloria Steinem*

And that means having enough blue-sky time to figure out what that means. To you—not to your kids, not to your husband. So you see, it really is *All About You*—a person you have chosen to be. The ultimate act of your life will be choosing what is right for you. You are the only person who can decide those issues, and isn't that exciting? Let's get started.

I dwell in Possibility.

—*Emily Dickinson*

# Chapter 2

# Identity Theft

*Help! I've been robbed!*
*I know the culprit;*
*he's bald, chubby, and completely adorable.*
*But the little thief stole my identity.*

 $\mathcal{W}$e hear reports of identity theft every day. We even set up a toll-free hotline for women to call in to. It's our radio show. Women call with questions and stories about how to recover their stolen identities. Apparently, identity theft is common. So, if you're feeling at a loss, join the club. Some women report stories of being robbed by twins and even triplets. These women have spent the past twenty, thirty, to forty years working on their identity, only to have it altered forever with one small miracle: birth.

Let's face facts: when you become a mom, your identity changes. Life as you knew it is over. That's good and it's also very challenging. It's good because you will know a love like no other. It's challenging because perceptions change. Your becoming a mother changes the way your husband perceives you, it changes the way you perceive yourself, and it even changes the way the world perceives you. And here's the real tricky part about identity theft: no one prepares you for it because they can't. It's something you have to experience for yourself.

# HOW TO SPOT IDENTITY THEFT

**Your name is not your own.**

> I remember getting ready for a party. My husband and I were going out and it had been months since we had had a date night. I was fussing in front of the mirror (check that, I was trying to fuss in front of the mirror) when my two sons came running through my bathroom, fighting. One went in front of me, the other behind, and my lip liner went up my nose. They were yelling, "Mom, make him stop! Mom!" Then my daughter came prancing by in her princess Halloween costume and asked, "Mom, will you zip my dress, and can I have a chocolate milk?" Meanwhile, the two boys were still yelling "Mom!" I looked at my husband and said, "I'm changing my name to Dad." —Tami

**Your body is not your own.**

You stand naked in front of the mirror (if you dare) and wonder, Whose body is that?

> I'm not the body I used to be. My body is me and I don't recognize me anymore. I stand in front of the mirror trying to figure out what happened to my figure and it's all just a blur. I see other moms who are fit, toned, and even have younger children. They got their bodies back a heck of a lot quicker. My youngest is already in the first grade and I'm still struggling. I'm tired of struggling. —Ellie

What can be said about this? We have gone through physical changes that we never suspected. Many of us gained weight. We may have lost inches here, only to see them pop up there. Some of us have even experienced physical changes in the size of our feet and the color and texture of our hair. Our internal organs have even shifted. Did you know that childbirth affects the bottom of your vaginal wall?

**Your memory vanishes into thin air.**

> *It's actually a good thing they call me Mom because I can't even seem to remember anymore who I am.* —Kristine

You can't remember why you went upstairs or opened the refrigerator. You stand there staring, hoping something will jump out at you.

**Your schedule is not your own.**

> *I'm an employee: an employee of my boss, of my kids, of my husband, and to top it off I'm an unpaid volunteer at the school. Everyone has a plan for my day, everyone except for me.* —Trina

You probably didn't realize when you said, "I do," that you meant, "I'll do for everyone forever."

**Your time is not your own.**

> *I finally found time for myself, then they found me.* —Drew

We hear from women who lock themselves in closets, bathrooms; we even heard from a woman hiding in the garage. Women are desperate for more time in the day, more time to exercise, to organize, to read a magazine, or to just sit in silence.

**Your energy is spent on everyone else.**

> *I thought energy converted into calories. With all the emotional and physical energy I expend on everyone else, I should be losing weight and not burning out.* —Courtney

Running errands, lifting loads of laundry, jumping through hoops at work—it's no wonder we fall into bed praying our husband doesn't have energy either.

## IN PRAISE OF MOTHERHOOD

We understand the need to maintain unique identities through careers, hobbies, politics, and opinions, but the greatest change in our identity happened the moment we became mothers. That is the moment we truly understood unconditional love, what it felt like to be more scared than ever before and in the same moment stronger than ever. Motherhood can bring us to our knees, and it can send us to the heavens. It is who we are, and we should bathe in its splendor. We must use it to become even stronger, more compassionate, empathetic, wiser, and energized.

Now that your identity journey has begun, it's time to start looking at the many culprits of identity theft. Although an identity theft occurred when you became a mother, your children aren't to blame. The real culprits are still at large. So, let's now start to identify the real thieves.

## THE REAL IDENTITY THIEVES

Will the real identity thieves please step forward? Ladies, meet the lineup:

**Labels**
**Depression**
**Exhaustion**
**Guilt**

These are the true culprits. These are the thieves that rob us of our positive attitudes, strength, energy, and joy. These are the gremlins that berate us and continually point out our weaknesses, fears, and failures. These thieves hit each and every one of us at some time or another. Sometimes they sneak in and out of our lives so quickly they hardly leave a trace. Other times they hit like gangbusters, wreaking havoc in our lives. Their timing can also be unpredictable. The good news is, however, that each of these thieves can be stopped, and we're going to share some strategies to put an end to the crime spree.

## LABELS

Soccer moms, stay-at-home moms, working moms, and any other mom who has been the target of labeling is familiar with this problem; in some way or another that includes all of us. We say this because the media love to put labels on us. We're even guilty of doing it to each other. But the truth is we never hear anyone call a dad a "soccer dad" or a "working dad." We believe we moms do it to each other because from the time we were little girls, we spent a lot of time trying to fit in, to find a group we could belong to. It's no different now that we're all grown up. But just as labeling can be bad on the playground, labeling can also be detrimental in the parking lot.

Labels rob us of our identity. When we were stay-at-home moms, we weren't just SAHMs. Now that we're working moms, we're not just some WAHMs. The same is true for you. No matter if you're working or staying home (which is still working, in our book), you are more than what either of those labels may attach to you. The key is to identify what makes you unique, not just to settle for words that lump you into some group.

## Quickies

Here are some quick ways to shake your social labels.

1. Stop labeling yourself. Don't think of yourself as a SAHM, working mom, or soccer mom.
2. Make a list of your passions, interests, and qualities that make you unique. Post the list somewhere you know you'll see it every day as a reminder.
3. Picture yourself in a variety of roles. For example, Mary will picture herself singing, Heather will picture herself dancing. What are some fun and active things you picture yourself doing?
4. Try new things. Take classes, read, paint, play music.
5. Talk about the new things you're trying. Tell your husband, kids, and friends. Ask them about their interests. This kind of positive dialogue builds momentum and enthusiasm for you and your loved ones.

# DEPRESSION

Depression is a serious issue for women and one we should be talking about more readily and more openly. The truth is many of us have gone through it. In some cases it's more severe than in others. Depression can range anywhere from the baby blues to thoughts of suicide. Postpartum depression has not been adequately studied, but doctors estimate that up to 20 percent of all women experience some symptoms. In fact, according to the National Institute of Mental Health (NIMH):

> Women experience depression about twice as often as men. Many hormonal factors may contribute to the increased rate of depression in women particularly such factors as menstrual cycle changes, pregnancy, miscarriage, postpar-

tum period, premenopause, and menopause. Many women also face additional stresses such as responsibilities both at work and home, single parenthood, and caring for children and for aging parents.

For more information visit the NIMH website at www.nimh.nih.gov/home.htm.

## Resources
Postpartum Support International, www.postpartum.net
UCLA Pregnancy and Postpartum Mood Disorders Program,
    www.npi.ucla.edu/center/mood/rs_pregnancy.html
American Psychiatric Association, www.psych.org

# EXHAUSTION

Moms are tired. We're exhausted because our sleep is interrupted and we don't log enough hours in bed. We're also exhausted because we're trying to juggle too many tasks at once. We have obligations at home, at work, and at the school. We're stressed trying to manage the finances, do the grocery shopping, run the errands, all while wondering if we're good moms. Most mothers are too exhausted dealing with the minute-to-minute problems and duties of daily life in the present to envision a different future. We can't even begin to think about living a passionate life when we're wiped out.

> When I was pregnant with my first baby, my girlfriends who were already mothers used to joke that I would never sleep again. They were wrong. My son just went to college and I slept all last week.
> —Marilyn

That's fantastic news if you don't have children under the age of eighteen. But for those of us with a decade or two to go, we need more immediate solutions. That's why on our radio show we turn to sleep expert Davis Ehrler. Davis is a postpartum doula (a birthing coach) and infant/child sleep consultant.

Here are her ten tips on how moms can get a better night's sleep:

1. Establish an age-appropriate bedtime routine for your children. Be consistent with this so your evening can have order and enjoyment.
2. Exercise early in the day if a late afternoon workout keeps you awake at night.
3. Take some downtime when you are overwhelmed. It's really okay to close your bedroom door and breathe.
4. Choose a time that you are officially "off the clock." Try 9 p.m. Stop working (housework and outside work) and begin to decompress before bedtime.
5. Eliminate caffeine in the evening.
6. Take a warm bath with lavender essential oil.
7. Drink a warm cup of chamomile tea.
8. Read for ten to twenty minutes.
9. Write five things you are most grateful for each night. What a great way to end your day! Sleeping children might top the list each night.
10. Write in your journal. Let it all out, girl.

Think about this. You don't let your kids stay up late because you know they need their sleep. Fact is, you do too. Most of us need at least eight hours a night to stay healthy and on top of our game.

For more information visit Davis's website at www.3daysleep solution.com.

# GUILT

Overwhelmingly, when we talk with other women, we hear a lot of guilt, worry, and self-blame. Guilt robs us of our confidence, energy, and productivity. We're too often busy chastising ourselves over things that don't really matter or we can't change anyway.

Take a look at just a few of the e-mails we get daily on the subject of guilt:

- My husband has no idea how much debt we're in and I'm afraid to tell him because I feel responsible.
- I feel guilty that I'm not spending enough time focused on my children.
- I'm staying with my husband because of the kids. I'd feel too guilty if I asked him to move out.
- I feel guilty that my marriage didn't work out and how it's affecting the kids.
- I feel guilty for spending too many hours at work.
- I feel guilty that I'm not cooking enough nutritious meals for my family.
- I feel guilty that my home looks like a tornado swept through it.
- I feel guilty that the laundry is piling up.
- I feel guilty that I can't stick to my diet or exercise routine.
- I can't stop shopping. We don't have the money, but I still whip out the credit cards. I end up hiding the items or returning them.
- I feel guilty that our family photos are still in boxes.

That is a painful amount of guilt to swallow silently and alone. Guilt is a state of mind. You start to eliminate guilt when you start changing the way you think. So, here are some tips on how to start relieving the burden of guilt.

## Guilt-relieving Quickies

Think positive thoughts.

Don't procrastinate. Guilt keeps growing when you're constantly thinking about what you should be doing, rather than just doing something. Do one thing now.

It's okay to say no and you don't need any excuses. There is no
need to explain or justify your answer.

You are not an island. When you have a family, you have a team.
Ask for help. Ask your husband for help with the finances.
Ask your kids for help folding the clothes.

Schedule a girls' night out. The conversation and laughter you
share with girlfriends is a great way to erase guilty feelings.

Go out on a date. Don't feel guilty about leaving your kids with
Grandma and Grandpa or a trusted sitter. Kids are comforted
seeing their parents having fun together.

Scheduling workouts refuels us. It's even better when we actually
work out.

And a good pedicure is heaven. Not to mention a facial, a
manicure, and/or a massage. These are pleasures, not guilty
pleasures. Enjoy getting pampered.

Warding off the gremlins all begins with fundamental self-care.
Mother the mother. Give yourself all of the advice, love, and care you
give to your kids and to others. Start doing what you know is good for
you and you'll no longer feel like a victim of identity theft. In fact,
you'll start feeling like there's a new sheriff in town.

\* \* \*

We believe identity theft, while at first feeling like a crime, can lead us
to an opportunity like no other. Motherhood gives you strength, and it
changes you on a primal level. You discover unconditional love, a love
that makes you stronger than you knew was possible. Motherhood
gives you greater access to your soul.

**So, don't think theft. Think evolution.**

Becoming a mother is a rite of passage. With your motherly in-
sights you are poised to evolve to your highest potential. This evolution is made possible by your children. Becoming a mother changes

you in the most soul-wrenching way. It's hard to imagine or even re-member who you were before you had them. Recognizing this trans-formation is the first step in the evolution of your unique identity. There are other steps we have learned along the way in the identity evolution:

- **You grow as they grow.** As your children mature, so does your identity. Who you are today is not who you will be in twenty years.
- **Be proactive in your evolution.** You are evolving whether you want to or not. You can't become complacent. Take this rich opportunity to stretch boundaries and comfort levels. This is the time to try new things.
- **Count your blessings every day** (and more than once a day if possible). You have people in your life who will love you unconditionally and want the best for you.
- **Recognize your ability to inspire.** You are an inspiration to your children, your friends, and your family.

How do you grow? How do you seize that rich opportunity to go outside your comfort zone, and how do you actually inspire others? We've asked ourselves these questions on numerous occasions. Life coaches and experts have told us repeatedly to put ourselves first. And we believe in the idea. We believe that to take care of our children, we must take care of ourselves first. Realistically, however, it's nearly im-possible to always put ourselves first. And to be quite honest, we don't know a single mom who does it often enough.

Here's the truth. We find ourselves putting our families first. We feed the kids before we feed ourselves; we skip our workout to shuttle kids to soccer practice or ballet; we spend our time at work, helping with homework, making dinner, and then cleaning the kitchen, finish-ing chores.

Under these circumstances, how do you stretch your boundaries, take risks, and still be a good parent? And then, how do you do it without feeling guilty for taking time and attention away from your family? Is it selfish to want your own identity? The answer, of course, is no. However, the reality of what it takes to achieve a new and unique identity can be elusive.

It's elusive because most of us can't put our finger on what it is our soul is craving. We know there is something more for us; we just can't grab it. So, we busy ourselves day in and day out with our chores and responsibilities, sometimes doing them happily and other times begrudgingly. This is a fact, and it's a trigger point in our identity evolution. When we're just going through the motions, it's time for change. Start with one small step or with our list of Identity Quickies.

## Identity Quickies

1. Make a list of all the things that you're hoping to have or to experience in your life. Let the list be as long as it needs to be.

2. Now, choose one thing off the list. Something that rings your bell and gets you excited about finding a pocket of time to work on it. Whatever you choose doesn't have to be some grand undertaking. It just has to get you started.

3. Find a half-hour pocket of time you can grab. Is it the half hour after dropping off the kids at school, the half hour during your lunch hour, or the half hour before bed? Finding a pocket of time to stop your world and focus on yourself is necessary. That half hour might be as simple as a walk, a journaling exercise, or research on a potential business idea. The key is that this pocket of time is yours.

4. Expect there to be times when you feel uninspired and lack motivation. That's okay. At this point, you need to

be recharged. Turn up the music, get outside, go for a walk, burn some candles, or cozy up with a good book.

This process has worked for us and for others. It's important to point out that we're not trying to invent identities that are independent of our children. In fact, our families are an integral facet of what makes each of us unique.

# A MOTHER CAN ONLY BE AS HAPPY AS HER MOST UNHAPPY CHILD

A good friend—and this friend is a father—made an observation that we will carry with us forever. Jules tells us what happens whenever their grown children call the house. If his wife, Yael, answers the phone, he can tell immediately by watching the expressions on her face and the tone in her voice how their children are feeling. He also says it doesn't end with the phone call. If one child is sad, his wife is sad.

There is so much wisdom in this statement. The day we became mothers, our identities changed forever. When we took on the responsibility of raising other people, our identity became absorbed in those people. Our children shape us. Their joys, their sorrows, their anxieties, their confidence become our own. When they hurt, we hurt. When they're happy, we rejoice. This is not "living through our children." This is living with our children. Each child is a part of our soul, and our soul is our identity. We must embrace our identity as mothers.

---

Women marry men, hoping they'll change; men marry women, hoping they won't—and they're both wrong.

—*Folk wisdom*

---

At the birth of their first child, friends of ours received a card that read "Congratulations on the new addition to your family." Inside the card: "Life as you knew it is now over."

Wow! It didn't take very long for them to realize the truth of that statement.

At first our friend was a bit offended. Then we suggested she reread the card and at the end of the last sentence add, " . . . and what an opportunity."

**"Life as you knew it is now over—and what an opportunity."**

We're not trying to be corny, rah-rah, self-affirming, nauseating cheerleaders. But we do, as much as possible, try to remind ourselves that our children deserve mothers who are excited to have them in their lives. Children deserve mothers who are also excited about their own lives.

We realize, however, that as much positive talk as we try to inject into our daily routine, our mom identity and the search for a new unique identity can be overwhelming.

In theory, we had nine months to think about it. As typical mothers, however, our thoughts during those nine months were happy fantasies about babies, about seeing our children grow, about the fun we would share as a family. When reality set in—as it does quickly—we hardly knew what hit us. There is no question that all new mothers experience a life change that is both overwhelming and difficult to manage. The new responsibilities to the family, to the school, to the home, to a husband, and to an incredibly busy life often leave new mothers with no time to plan, no time to dream, no time to remember who they were, and certainly no time to think about their futures. When we are swamped with immediate problems—and we all are—it is difficult to have a vision of the future.

Hopelessness and depression are frequently the most extreme manifestations of this problem.

When women are depressed, they eat or go shopping. Men invade another country. It's a whole different way of thinking.

—*Elayne Boosler*

# EVOLVING FROM WHO WE WERE TO WHO WE WANT TO BE

The Unique You isn't going to emerge full-blown from some other planet. She's going to be based on who you were, the good parts of who you are now, and your vision of who you want to be.

In order to focus on the Unique You, you have to look back on the woman you have been. Your "herstory" tells you that with each decade, you have evolved. The woman you were in your twenties is not who you are today. Although you might want your twenty-year-old abs or thighs, you don't want your twenty-year-old insecurities. You also realize on this road to the woman you are becoming that in the past you may have been too self-absorbed, had too much to drink, slept with too many men, and stayed up too late. You even had the nerve to judge mothers who couldn't control their screaming children. (Of course that was before you became a mother!)

You used to have all the answers, and now you have all the questions. You recognize you still stay up too late, but now you're finishing a project for work or nursing a baby instead of carousing and dancing on the tables. (But, girlfriend to girlfriend, let's admit a little table-top cha-cha-cha is something we miss.)

Here are some of the other things the MomsTown women tell us that they miss from their former lives:

I miss the throwdown. That can't-rip-the-clothes-off-fast-enough kind of sex. You know, the adrenaline rush of unadulterated passion. That's what I miss. —Tracy

I miss flirting. I miss making eyes with the cute guy across the bar and the way he looked at me and how I pretended not to notice him. —Julie

I miss big hair. I took to heart the bigger the hair, the closer to heaven. I miss teasing; I miss mousse; I miss the two hours I had to actually fuss over my hair. —Candace

I miss love songs. The love songs that spoke to my broken heart, my melodramatic feelings of love and that I couldn't go on without him or that feeling that he couldn't go on without me. —Mia

So let's figure out how to take the best parts of your old life and reshape them to fit into the Unique You!

## MomsTown Take on the Past

How to turn the memories of your former life into part of your daily reality:

- Look at old photographs.
- Talk to a parent, family member, or childhood friend about your memories of each other.
- Put your own childhood pictures in frames and display them with other pictures.
- Start a journal about the things you used to love as a little girl. Did you love music, dance, or horses? Whatever your favorite pastimes, write them down, even if they were just childhood dreams.

- Also in your journal, write about the people you most admired or respected as a child. Who were they? What did they do? What did they look like? And how did they treat you? Discover what it is about those people that makes you remember them.

Now that we've explored some techniques for reviving the parts of the old you that you miss, let's take a look at revving up some RPMs for the Unique You.

# IDENTITY RPMS

**Research**
**Pursue**
**Move**

If fulfilling the woman you want to become involves enriching your knowledge of art history, playing chamber music, traveling through Provence, creating pastries, taking up golf, spinning wool, writing prose, or making jewelry, then you look to the RPMs. In creating our new identity, we have these three essential steps.

First, do your **research.** Research is important because you have to get past the fantasy to see if your dream passes muster. Sometimes, having a dream is like meeting a man. At first, he looks great and seems to be a perfect match. Then with a little research, you quickly come to the conclusion that maybe this man isn't for you after all. So. If you thought you wanted to move your family to Tuscany lock, stock, and barrel, in search of a simpler, purer lifestyle, you should do your research. You research the reality of living in Tuscany.

Then it's time to **pursue.** In transforming yourself, you have to become accustomed to pursuing. This is a change: women have been taught over the years to sit back and be pursued. In matters of the heart, that may work, but in matters of your future, you must become the pursuer. You have to take the initiative, admit what you want, and move toward it. You might be worlds apart from your male counterparts, but there is something we all have in common. There is a thrill in the pursuit; we love to be working toward something. It gives us purpose.

And finally, you **move.** You'll find this is a recurring theme. We have found that whatever project we're working on, whether it's for work, home, or the garden, we must move. You must move your body to move your mind.

## THE FIVE-STEP IDENTITY DANCE

Let's begin the process of finding your uniqueness by getting you ready to dance!

1. What do you miss about the old you? What are your memories, fantasies—fun stuff, and fulfilling stuff that you'd like to have again? Just jot down a short list.
2. What are the good parts of your present life? Write them down and think about how they could be enlarged.
3. Who are some of the girlfriends from your past with whom you have lost touch? Can you find them again? Start with one. Maybe there is a night out or a coffee klatch in your future.
4. Who are some of the women you have met recently with whom you may share a lot of similar issues? Reach out to one of them. You may both be surprised at how comforting and supportive it is to find someone who understands.
5. Let yourself go. Pull down the shades, turn up the music, and take three minutes to let go. Trust us: it feels good; it's liberating; it will put you in the mood to search for a Unique

You. And after a while you just may find you don't even have to draw the shades. Heck, let the neighbors watch!

*I have two kids, a husband, and a job I don't really enjoy. I got married in my twenties, had kids right away, and I used to feel like I left my future behind me. That is, until I woke up one night and decided I'm going back to school. I'm getting my degree entirely online. I'm so excited.* —Tory, in a post on our Moms-Town.com forum

Tory is dancing her own dance. Like Tory, when you complete the Five-Step exercise by letting your imagination run wild, you get an opportunity to see yourself in a new way. Keeping this in mind, consider some of the funny, practical, and inspirational ways MomsTown members are letting themselves go. For example, one mom bought a motorcycle and started a hiking club for women. Another, afraid of the water, took up surfing. A thirty-nine-year-old friend is tapping her way into a new identity, and another is pirouetting. Nothing like a forty-year-old in toe shoes!

Identity is defined as "the condition of being oneself and not another." Being you, enhancing your unique identity is a gift. It's a gift you give to yourself and to everyone who comes into contact with you. We trust that you are teaching your children to stand up for themselves, think for themselves, and be true to their souls. When you stand up to labeling, depression, exhaustion, and guilt, you begin to eliminate the power of identity thieves. In essence, you take back your power and unleash creative energy so that you can finally act on your potential. You still have a lot of living to do. You are not a finite production. And—here's the really cool part—who you are today (your now identity) is going to keep evolving, and who you'll be in ten or twenty years from now will also change. Look forward to it, cherish your evolution, and continue to look at every day as a new gift, a new day to live to your fullest.

*Chapter 3*

# Resetting Your Clock

"*W*hy is it there's an *I* and *me* in *time*, but no time for me?" Our friend Kathryn was joking when she asked us about how to get more time in her day. In all seriousness, Kathryn hustles all morning to get the kids off to school; she packs lunch, prepares breakfast, organizes backpacks, drives the kids to the school, and, maybe, has a few quick moments to grab a coffee before she heads into the office. She's a mortgage broker, and as soon as she gets to work, she is handling files, making calls, and trying to close deals.

At the end of her "workday" she hops in the car to begin her next shift. She immediately starts thinking about what's for dinner, and how many errands she has to squeeze in before picking the kids up at after-school care, and when the heck will she have an hour to work out? She told us, "I really need to start walking during my lunch *half hour*."

> The bad news is time flies. The good news is you're the pilot.
>
> —*Michael Altshuler*

Kathryn's story of being time-jammed is serious and sincere. Worse yet, Kathryn is Everymom. Running short on time is a problem all mothers face every day. It doesn't matter if you work outside the home or work at home; you always seem to be wishing you had another hour in the day.

## FOUR QUICK LESSONS ABOUT MANAGING TIME

Forget owning a house and having a fat bank account, the *real* American dream is managing your time and getting organized. Most of us think that if we could somehow figure out how to fit it all into one day, we'd be golden. If we could manage the kids, manage the husband, manage the household, and look like a million bucks doing it, wouldn't we be fabulous! Well, guess what? We tried all that and have learned four big lessons after falling flat on our faces.

### Lesson #1:
#### KIDS DON'T WANT TO BE MANAGED

We put a lot of pressure on ourselves thinking we have to manage every aspect of our kids' lives. The truth is most kids just want to hang out at home and play. Why is it we feel like we're better mothers when we have the kids overscheduled? Do we really think raising busy little bees will one day make them the queen bees?

Lesson #2:

## HUSBANDS REALLY, REALLY DON'T WANT TO BE MANAGED

We have found that when we approach our family schedules as a team, we get more accomplished and get our priorities to mesh, and no one feels like they're being led around by the nose or forced into doing something they don't want to do.

Lesson #3:

## MORE IN THE HOUSEHOLD, MORE TO MANAGE

Too many toys, too much paper, too many things lead us to a house out of control. We might not be ready to toss the toy box or our closet of clothes in the donation bin, but letting go of our attachment to so much stuff is a great first step.

Lesson #4:

## WE AGE MORE WHEN WE RUN AROUND WITH OUR HAIR ON FIRE

Stress leads to all kinds of emotions that are harmful to our waistlines and our face lines. We also recognize we're not that attractive to others when we're rushing. Rushing past others says to them that they're not that important, that we don't have time for them. How beautiful is that?

# SOME TIMELY TRUTHS

Happily, our MomsTown moms have come to the rescue with loads of commonsense advice and tips to help their time-starved friends. Some of these ideas we have organized into "rules" and some we are delivering fresh from e-mails or the radio airwaves. First, however, we want to take a look at the time problem and explain why it affects us so powerfully.

We were asked to help out Tara, a busy mom of two, for a TV show. Tara had sent an e-mail to the show's producers pleading for help. She didn't even have enough time in the day to get dressed before taking her kids to school. In fact, we surprised her at the school and caught her in her pajama sweats. She was a bit shocked, to say the least, and her daughter turned about seven shades of red when her mom stepped out of the car looking as if she just rolled out of bed. Tara told us she simply didn't have time in the morning to get dressed. She says she barely even had time to get the kids fed, get lunches packed, and get the kids to school on time. Tara says she's always running late and that the clock is always ticking against her.

Once Tara dropped off the kids, we went back to her house. We asked her to recreate her morning routine, and we quickly noticed several time-savers she was just skipping over.

1. She admitted that her husband offered her help on several occasions, and she refused the help, saying, "No, I can handle it." When people offer help, for crying out loud, take it. Accepting help and asking for help, especially from your husband, is nothing to be ashamed of. It's also not a slap in the face when they offer help. Tara's husband wasn't offering help because he thought she was incapable; he just wanted to help his wife. Here's a little secret: men love independent women but they also want to know they're needed. We're pretty sure it's in their chemical makeup to want to be the hero.

2. She wasn't starting her day the night before. It's imperative when you're a busy mom to get as many head starts as possible. Our first head start of the day starts twelve hours prior. We make sure that the kids' clothes are picked out (whether we do it or they do it), shoes are lined up with socks tucked in them, homework is in the backpacks, and

as much of the lunch as possible is already packed. We also choose our outfits for the next day, and if we don't think we'll have time to shower in the morning (though skipping it is not recommended simply because a morning shower is therapeutic), we bathe at night.

3. Tara also loves sleeping in and made a habit out of hitting the snooze button one too many times. Every tap of the snooze set her morning back another ten minutes. As nice as it may be to sleep in, when we do it, it sets the tone for the day. Snooze buttons are a bad idea. We are telling ourselves we just aren't ready to face the day. We're better off when that alarm goes off if we get up and get going. The act gives us that mental cue that we are awake, energized, and ready for anything.

4. Tara was putting a lot of energy into the details and missing the big picture. She put the pressure on herself to iron her daughter's clothing every morning. This is a nice touch but probably unnecessary every day. Most clothes today look great right out of the dryer (but the trick is not to let them sit in the dryer for hours or even days). Getting laundry out of the dryer, folded, hung, and put away promptly saves the step of having to iron everything. Remember, a time-saving tip is to handle items as few times as possible. This goes not just for the laundry but also for mail, toys, and dishes.

By putting just a few time-savers into play, Tara was able to start her day in a better frame of mind.

In our conversation with Tara and the hundreds of others who have sent us e-mails, we have come to realize a few timely truths.

**If you had another hour in the day, you would probably just fill it with more of what you're already doing.**

You'd just cram more of the same errands, cleaning, and work you're already doing into that extra time. There's a reason why it's said, "Habits are hard to break." And believe it or not, working out how you handle dinnertime, the way you shop, and even the route you take to school and to work is all about the habits you have developed. Unless you are prepared to change your habits, you'll continue to be caught in this time conundrum.

**You can't *make* time. You can only *take* it.**

The key is not to let it take you over. You want to know how to take care of yourself, your family, your career, and still have fun. The following TIME formula will help you manage your overscheduled, overstressed, overwhelming life:

**Think** about your day: Try to look at the big picture. Each day is a new opportunity to get tasks completed and an opportunity to do something fun, maybe even something memorable. When you're thinking about the day, don't just think about the long list of to-dos. Try to think about how you're going to enjoy your time throughout the day.

**Initiate** action: Start each day with a clear purpose and direction. Move out smartly, as the marines say. There will be surprises that will take you off course, but don't abandon your mission, even if you have to complete your goal the next day. Following through on goals, no matter how small or large, gives you a sense of accomplishment, and that feels good.

**Motivate** Get moving. Some days you wake up and you're just exhausted. When we wake up not quite ready to face the day, we just get going. We find that starting one task immediately in the morning gets our blood flowing. It might be as simple as starting a load of laundry. It sets the wheels of motivation in motion. So, if you're not feeling motivated, get moving.

**Embrace** the day: Let's not get too sappy about it, but each day of your life is unique and will never happen again. Focus on the positive. Try to never have a bad day. Of course, we know there will be bad moments during the day, but try to avoid making the whole day bad. Focus on the good in your day and not the bad. You can do this by embracing time, enjoying time, and focusing on your positive attitude.

---

Regret for wasted time is more wasted time.

—*Mason Cooley,*
O, The Oprah Magazine, *April 2004*

---

Remember, the goal of time management is to take the pressure off. To rush through life with guilt and panic because your plate is overflowing doesn't help you or anyone else. When you're rushing through your day, not taking the time to say hello or flash a warm smile, everyone and everything becomes a potential obstacle, in the way of your agenda. Take charge of your time, but remember that everyone else's time is also precious.

---

Half our life is spent trying to find something to do with the time we have rushed through life trying to save.

—*Will Rogers*

---

# TWENTY TIME-KILLING HABITS AND HOW TO CHANGE THEM

1. Skipping breakfast. This is the number-one time killer. The best way to manage time is with your physical and mental energy. If we don't supply our body with proper nutrition, we're sure to run out of energy and time.

2. Thinking you have no time. If you think it, you're right. Perception is reality. If you keep telling yourself you don't have enough time in the day, then you'll never have it. Change the way you talk to yourself about time and you'll find time will start working in your favor.

3. Feeling guilty about things you didn't get done. Fact is, sometimes stuff doesn't get done. Let it go. Worrying about everything we should have done doesn't help us get tasks accomplished now. Guilt works against us and promotes procrastination.

4. Surfing the Internet. This may sound ironic coming from a couple of Internet talk show hosts, but we know so many women (including ourselves) who spend way too much time online. A good way to break this habit is to get up from your desk chair once every ten to fifteen minutes. A little break from the monitor will break the online trance, and it's good for your booty.

5. Starting the day without a plan. Our goal is to write down the plan for our day the night before. It doesn't always work out that way, but when it does, it's great. We are able to wake up with a game plan in our head and a list to keep us on track.

6. Grocery shopping and running errands without a list. We know we save at least fifteen minutes every time we go into the grocery store with a list. Plus it saves us money. When we wander the aisles wondering what we need, we waste time and buy unnecessary items.

7. Not keeping task lists. To-do lists can be a pain in the patoot, but they are necessary to keep time on our side. We've found a couple of great websites that help us organize our lists.

## Resources for
### TO-DO LISTS

www.ListOrganizer.com. With 140 lists for everything from laundry to financial issues, this site makes it a cinch to solve your to-do list problems for $11.95 per year.

www.Printablelists.com. This is a terrific site for online help in almost every area of to-do lists imaginable. We love the range of grocery lists on this site and the many useful related links they offer on the topic of "organize." And it is all free.

8. Not keeping a priority list. This is a list of things that need to get done immediately or as soon as possible. Go back to your to-do list and prioritize your tasks. As tasks get completed, check them off, and as things come up, add them. This priority list could be kept in your purse or posted in a place where you'll see it every day.

9. Multitasking. Try, as hard as it may be, not to multitask. As women, we pride ourselves on being able to juggle a dozen things at one time. Truth be told, we're better off doing one thing at a time. It's simply more efficient to accomplish at least one task in its entirety than to have a dozen unfinished projects sitting on your desk.

10. Not using time wisely. Our kids get marks at school for how they utilize time. At the end of the day we try to look back and grade ourselves on how we utilized our time. This reflection gives us clues on how we could do better tomorrow, or if we've earned a day to play hooky.

11. Leaving stuff without a home. Give the stuff in your home a home. We'll discuss this concept a bit more in our "A River Runs Through It" chapter, but basically when things are put away where they belong, we save time when looking for them. Create a home for keys, jackets, shoes, mail, bills paid, and bills owed. This will save you minutes, if not hours, of frustration and anxiety.

12. Making every day a grind. Carve out time during each day to enjoy something simple: a walk with your kids, watching the sunset, or sitting and doing nothing for even just a few moments.

13. Talking on the phone. When on the phone, concentrate on the phone call, and give yourself a defined period of time to chat. It also helps to stand up when you're on the phone. If you're sitting or doing something else during the call, you're more apt to spend more time than you wanted on the phone.

14. Walking through the world without an organizer. Get an organizer and use it. If you already use one, buy some new pages to freshen it up. It'll give you a new zest when it comes to managing your calendar.

15. Lugging around extra weight. Clean out all the junk in your purse and your car weekly.

16. Not using waiting time. This is the time you spend in the car waiting for the kids at school or during an extracurricular activity, in line at the bank, or in the reception room at the doctor's office. Carry your organizer with you to jot down notes or more dreaded to-dos!

17. Procrastinating. When you put something off for a later time, you inevitably waste more time stressing out about how you'll get it done later. It's much quicker to just do it and get it over with.

18. Not telling it like it is. If you don't have time for a project or a committee, then say so. The reality is there is only so much

time in a day and you are one person. Don't think taking on more than your fair share is going to make you a better person or a better mom. It'll just cause you more stress, and the people around you will notice the stress before they notice the insurmountable number of tasks you've committed to.

19. Not listening to your biorhythms. Most of us have certain times of the day when we're more alert. For example, many of us are better able to handle difficult tasks in the morning. By the afternoon, our energy level drops. This is the time of day we should save for follow-ups.

20. Always running late. This is a bad habit for two main reasons. First, when you're always running late, you're not in control of your time; it controls you. Second, it's disrespectful. Lateness is only fashionable at a cocktail party. When you're late to an appointment, you're telling that person that their time is not as important as yours, and that's just downright rude.

## MomsTown Tips
### ON TIME-SAVING QUICKIES

We asked the gals on our MomsTown.com forum for their favorite Quickies. Here's what they said:

*Sally from Encinitas*
Clean out the trunk of my car.
Balance the checkbook—or at least start it!
Reply to and send e-mails.
Mix up a box of cake mix and put it in the oven.

*Nikki from Memphis*
Empty the dishwasher.
Throw away junk mail/old magazines.

Write one thank-you note. (It's not all of them, but it's better
than none!)
Clean out the produce drawers in my fridge.


Barb from Phoenix
Make my customer contact list.
Water my plants.
Put together five information packets for my business.
Clean off the kitchen counter.


If you need help taking a Quickie break, go to MomsTown.com.
There we've got a Quickie task list. Just type in the stuff you wish to
get completed in a day, a week, or a month, and we will automatically
send you an e-mail reminder of your Quickie for the day.

---

Dost thou love life? Then do not squander time,
for that is the stuff life is made of.

—Benjamin Franklin

---

## MomsTown Tip
### ON INTERNET TIME

Computer, computer, computer. My Internet was down almost all
weekend and I got so many other things done that I really realized
how much time I was spending online. —Jody

# SEVEN RULES TO REPEAT

There's no doubt that you understand that you have time problems. Let's take a look at seven rules that have helped us get more done in a day, a week, a month, etc.

1. Phooey on balance.
2. Flex our ability.
3. Rhythm rocks.
4. Better done than perfect.
5. Quickies save the day.
6. Don't get caught inhaling.
7. We never know what's going on in someone else's world.

## MomsTown Rule #1:
### PHOOEY ON BALANCE

*What we believe in:*

---

Doing a thing well is often a waste of time.

—*Robert Byrne*

---

When you tune into our radio show, you'll hear the word "phooey" being tossed around—especially when anyone brings up the subject of a "balanced life." Apparently, magazine editors and life coaches believe balance is important and that to live a truly exemplary life, one must achieve it. Alas, you're never going to *balance* your life. Once you've admitted it and realized "balance" and "mom" don't belong in the same sentence, you should let it go. Life's not a perfectly balanced scale; it's more like a seesaw.

*How it works for us:*

There are going to be times when one of our kids is struggling with school and our focus needs to be with them and so we can't spend as much time at the office. Then a few months later, a coworker with a job we want resigns and we've got the chance to leap up the corporate ladder. That means giving our nine-to-five gig a little more attention and letting things at home slide a bit. (In the scheme of life, does it matter that our kids eat takeout three nights in a row? Or that the laundry isn't done?)

The specifics change as life changes, but what stays the same is the fact that we're on a seesaw. Parts of our lives are up high on the list, while others are down low. Then it swings the other way. But balanced it's not.

Anna Quindlen, the best-selling author and former *New York Times* columnist, once said, "You can have it all. You just can't have it all at the same time." Amen! That's what leads us to say phooey on balance. We don't believe in it. And we're not alone. It's okay not to believe in balance.

## MomsTown Rule #2:
### FLEX OUR ABILITY

*What we believe in:*

We believe in flexibility. When we think of flexibility, we like to think about Keanu Reeves in the movie *Matrix*. Remember those amazing scenes when he's dodging an endless stream of bullets from all directions and his rubber band–like body bends with incredible flexibility? As moms, we have bullets of busyness coming our way 24/7. When we're flexible, we're able to get out of the bullets' paths.

*How it works for us:*

By embracing flexibility, we're able to let go of the unrealistic expectations of others and ourselves. We ask others to help share the load. Flexibility is the goal. Sometimes, we have to repeat that mantra ten times to ourselves. Or we write it on a piece of paper and tape it to our mirror. (Mary even has it as her screen saver.) What works is giving ourselves permission to bend in more than one direction today, knowing full well tomorrow we'll be stretching ourselves the opposite way.

Flexibility doesn't mean lowering or compromising our standards. It's about having the ability to stretch the limits in a positive direction. We believe flexibility increases patience and tolerance, and it's the most fun when we position ourselves for great things to happen.

**Flexibility is taking advantage of the moment.**

Flexibility allows the rush of adrenaline to push us in directions we never thought possible.

## MomsTown Tips
### ON FLEXIBILITY

Here are posts from women who visit our MomsTown.com website about what it means to be "in the moment."

> Being in the moment is thirty seconds at the end of my shower when I'm clean but just not ready to get out. —Kelly

> Being in the moment for a mom is driving the car with no kids and not noticing the radio is turned off. —Monica

> Being in the moment is a delicious trip to the grocery store by yourself. —Julie

# MomsTown Rule #3:
## RHYTHM ROCKS

*What we believe in:*

We believe in the rhythm method. Don't worry; our rhythm method won't have you counting days on the calendar, wondering if you are adding more players to your team. We have found that when we focus on the rhythm of the day rather than the routine of the day, we get more accomplished, we're less stressed, and the day is more enjoyable.

*How it works for us:*

Rhythm allows us to be in control; routine puts the schedule in control. This is not to say we shouldn't have a routine or a schedule, but they start to break down when we have no rhythm. Routines are too rigid and too easily broken. Routines fall apart when we go out of town, our child has a soccer game, guests come to visit, or the holidays arrive. Recognize that each day may have its own unique rhythm, just like a great dance. We may know all the steps, but if we have no rhythm, we look like Elaine in the infamous *Seinfeld* episode. We need to remind ourselves that some days will be upbeat and out of control, while other days will be as smooth as a waltz.

---

We say we waste time, but that is impossible. We waste ourselves.

—*Alice Bloch*

---

## MomsTown Rule #4:
### BETTER DONE THAN PERFECT

*What we believe in:*

This little rule saves us—and lots of our friends and women who tune into our show or visit our website—from stress, anxiety, and procrastination. Repeating it, over and over, helps take away the pressure of having to do something perfectly. We've realized, much to our amazement, that we are not perfect. It's true! And when we had this big Aha! moment, we also realized that things don't have to be done perfectly, and we started to get a heck of a lot more done.

We'd like to say we're brilliant and we just thought up the *Better done than perfect* rule while sipping coffee one morning. The truth of the matter is we had to be hit over the head with it. We had a public relations gal once ask us for a proposal. She had a client that she thought would be a good match for us. All we needed to do was provide her with a document outlining how we envisioned our two companies working together. Simple. The company she represented was big, a household name.

Don't bother wondering if we got the job or not: we didn't even try. It's not that we didn't want to work with this company. We really did. It's not that we couldn't have used the business. We could have. We passed on the opportunity because we got intimidated by the notion of perfection. The proposal had to be dynamite, didn't it? Well, that just overwhelmed us, and the proposal didn't happen. We let a potentially lucrative deal slip through our fingers because we were afraid what we'd put together wouldn't be perfect. There's an *s* word for that, *stupid*. But at least you can learn from our stupidity. Our friend Karen did.

*How it works for us:*

Karen is a freelance writer who used to drive herself crazy as a perfectionist. If an editor she was doing an article for wanted two experts in a story, she'd interview ten. If the editor asked for one statistic, she'd give him five to choose from. She had fat files for every story because of all the research she did. Diligent? Yes. Driving herself nuts? Completely!

We suggested she consider "Better done than perfect." She didn't think much about it when we told her that, but she said days later that while proofreading another story for the tenth time, she thought of those words. She knew what she had on her computer screen was good. She also knew it was done. Maybe not perfect, but done. She decided that was it and e-mailed it to her editor. It was two days before her deadline and normally she would have spent that time doing more research just to confirm the research she'd already done, calling more people and editing. Would you know it, her editor loved it. No major revisions.

---

How we spend our days is, of course, how we spend our lives.

—*Annie Dillard*

---

"That simple phrase—'Better done than perfect'—was incredibly liberating," Karen says, and now it's written in bold on a Post-it stuck to her computer. The truth is most of us are really good at what we do; we just don't trust that fact. Agonizing about perfection is pointless anyway. Perfection is in the eyes of the beholder. What's perfect to one of us might not be perfect to the other.

Karen is not the only one chanting, "Better done than perfect." We have talked to hundreds of women who have made progress with this four-word, get-it-done-and-off-your-plate rule. Enjoy not being perfect; enjoy getting things done. When you embrace this rule, you take the pressure off, you reduce the stress, and you put yourself in a better position to take charge of your time.

# MomsTown Rule #5:
## QUICKIES SAVE THE DAY

*What we believe in:*

Ever done this? You decide that you're going to clean out your dresser. You take everything out of every drawer and start to go through it. You try on a few sweaters and rummage through that stack of bras. But after a while you're tired and don't feel like you've made any headway. So you say to yourself, "I'll have more time tomorrow." And so you stuff everything back where it came from, close the drawers, and feel worse than when you started. Or you plan to take a day to get organized. You mark it on the calendar. But when that day arrives, you push it back. We always do. After all, we can find dozens of other things to do with a day that are a heck of a lot more fun than getting organized.

Our theory on getting organized: let go of the idea of major overhauls and think Quickies. No, not the kind that would make our husbands happy; we're talking about fifteen minutes of getting organized, such as finally putting the winter clothes away for the summer, and there's always time for one. The way we figure it, if we can conceive a child in fifteen minutes or less, we can probably clean out a desk drawer. We've read all kinds of books on how to get organized, how to clean off our desk, scrub our sinks, and create a task list. Some of the tips work. Neither of us can go to sleep with dishes in the kitchen sink. Some tips don't. No matter how many times we read up on how to handle all the junk mail, we're still buried under piles of paper on the kitchen countertop and our desks.

*How it works for us:*

A Quickie is manageable. It's a small chunk of time that we can all find in a day. Even if that means getting up fifteen minutes earlier than normal or staying up fifteen minutes later. Or maybe you can do a Quickie in those fifteen minutes between appointments, those fifteen minutes between dropping one son at swimming and picking the other up at soccer. Wherever you are, you can have a Quickie: at home, in the car, at the office.

## MomsTown Rule #6:
### DON'T GET CAUGHT INHALING

*What we believe in:*

We're not reminiscing about some college party; we're remembering to breathe. Really breathe. We're talking about the moments when we consciously inhale and exhale.

Our friend Jackie lives in New York City, where she takes the subway to work. If she heard the train coming, her heart used to race, she would start sweating, and she would run down two flights of stairs, pushing past people just so she could get to the platform and make the train. Her rushing was risky since the steps in that station are notoriously steep and several people had taken really bad spills down them. Unfortunately, like the rest of us, Jackie was on the go-go-go.

One day her husband was taking the train with her. He noticed her rushing and said, "What's the worst thing that would happen if you just walked down the stairs?" "I'd miss the train," Jackie said. "And then what?" her husband asked. She paused. "I'd wait and another would come in a few minutes." As the words came out of her mouth, Jackie heard how stupid she sounded. She was racing through her life just to shave a few minutes off her day? Risking a big fall that would set her life back way more than a few minutes? Plus, those minutes of rushing and stressing out about a train set a tone for the rest of her day. Her whole day was frantic and harried. It was a blur and a rush. After that morning she put a halt to the rushing and putting herself in danger. It's still not easy for her to slow down, but this recovering rusher admits that those few minutes make her day calmer. She's not sweating up her work clothes or angrily pushing past other people. When she gets the urge to hurry, she tells herself, "There's always another train"—words that go beyond her a.m. commute.

We're like Jackie and so many women who get caught on the inhale. We forget to exhale, but that's the part that helps release our stress and tension. It keeps us alive. We've all heard an instructor tell us in yoga or an exercise class to exhale, and we've found that what works for us in exercise will work in organization. In order for our bodies and our schedules to work efficiently, we need to breathe. Too often we stuff our schedules so full of errands and to-dos that we forget to exhale.

*How it works for us:*

Leslie called in to our radio show while she was driving in her car. She came to the stoplight and her shoulders were tight. She had a firm grip on the steering wheel (that steering wheel wasn't going anywhere without her tightly wound fingers wrapped securely around it). She had been thinking about a project deadline, her in-laws coming into town, the cough her son had been fighting for three weeks, and what to make for dinner.

Then all of a sudden it hit her. She remembered us saying, "Don't get stuck on the inhale." She let out a big breath. Her shoulders dropped about three inches. She relaxed. With that one exhale she felt better; she felt more clearheaded and in control of her time. In that moment of clarity she decided to book her in-laws a hotel room.

## MomsTown Rule #7:
### WE NEVER KNOW WHAT'S GOING ON IN SOMEONE ELSE'S WORLD

*What we believe in:*

It's impossible to know what's happening in other people's lives.

*Why isn't Jamie calling me back? Did I do something wrong? Is she mad at me or avoiding me?*

*I submitted my project proposal two days ago and I haven't had a response from my boss. Does she like it, not like it; did someone submit a better idea?*

*I sent my sister an e-mail and she hasn't e-mailed me back. That was three days ago. What's going on with her?*

We believe that it's not possible to always know what's happening in someone else's world. Have you ever noticed that people don't always respond to or do things as quickly as you would like? We have. When they don't respond right away, our minds start to create all kinds of scenarios. We get upset, we get insecure, we get anxious, or we simply get our feelings hurt. And for what?

Sometimes people don't respond right away because they're busy too. Imagine that! It has absolutely nothing to do with you and everything to do with them. Instead of taking it personally when potential clients don't get back to us after reading our proposal, we just tell ourselves that we don't know what's going on in their world. It's possible they're going through a personal or professional struggle or simply haven't gotten to it on their to-do list.

*How it works for us:*

When we remind ourselves that everyone's agenda is not about our agenda, we take a lot of pressure, blame, and anxiety off our shoulders. This freedom from worry and trying to predict outcomes allows us to be more productive with the time at hand. What will be, will be.

So, how do we release that worry and anxiety and feeling that we would like to control everyone's responses? First, we actually repeat our rule, "We don't know what's going on in someone else's world." Then we redirect our focus to what we do have control over. We have control over the actions we complete in a day. We might do something as simple as sitting down and writing a long-overdue thank-you note. A lot of time is wasted wondering, worrying, and what-iffing. By letting go of the wonder, the worry, and the what-if, we get a lot done and feel a heck of a lot better.

Breathing gives us clarity. Quickies get tasks accomplished. Flexibility gives us a chance. Being done releases guilt. And remembering that our time is precious gives us perspective.

# TIME ZAPPERS

Let's take a look at everyday pitfalls that can cause you to waste time.

## Time Zapper: NO GAME PLAN

Not having a plan for your day, your week, and your month is a waste of time. If you don't have a plan—even a loose one—for what you want to get accomplished during the day, the day will whiz right on by and nothing will get done. Ellen is retired. She told us how much she used to get accomplished when her kids were in school and she worked full-time as a nurse. Now that she's retired with grown kids and no set schedule, the day gets past her and little gets done.

## Time Zapper: NEGATIVITY

Negative thoughts rob you of time and huge amounts of energy. At night, our friend Sue battles negativity by writing down all the negative thoughts she had that day. Then she jots something positive down next to each one. Her writing exercise helps her see the positive side of most situations and most people.

## Time Zapper: REHASHING

Women are great at this. We go over the past. We ruminate. We sit there thinking, "What if this" and "what if that." But you can what-if yourself into the ground and you still can't change the past. Our girlfriend Kelly has a great tip. The minute she starts doing this, she stops and asks herself, "What am I gaining by revisiting the past?" Usually the answer is nothing.

# ACTION MANAGEMENT

Let's take a phrase out of our vocabulary: *time management*. What the heck is time management anyway? You can't manage time; you can only manage what you *do* with your time. We call that *action management*. You're managing your actions. There are a lot of people and things all poised to suck hours and minutes from your day. If you let them—which most put-everyone-else-first women do—you end up with little time left over for yourself and the fun stuff in life. Isn't it funny—you always seem to find enough time to take care of your kids, your home, your husband, and your job, but at the end of the day you're still in need of a manicure, haircut, exercise class, or an hour with a good book.

# SHOULDS, NEEDS, WANTS, AND LOVES

Whenever we get that feeling that we don't have enough time in the day, we take out a pencil and a piece of paper and draw a line down the center of the page. We title the left-hand column "Wants & Loves" and the right-hand column "Shoulds & Needs." Then we write. This is a technique we learned from our business coach and friend, Mark LeBlanc. We list all the things we want and what we would love to experience in Wants & Loves, and then we list the things that we have to catch ourselves from feeling guilty about in Shoulds & Needs. This helps us focus on where our time goes in a day. And when we stop to think about it, each side exists because of the other. For example, if we want to take a vacation, we need to put away a few extra dollars. If we want to spend a morning shopping with a girlfriend, then we should say no to the mom asking us to man the bake sale table all week. Looking at it this way makes it easier to get the Shoulds & Needs accomplished with less stress.

| Wants & Loves | Shoulds & Needs |
|---|---|
| Take some quiet time. | Do the laundry. |
| Read a book. | Clean the kitchen sink. |
| Meditate. | Shop for groceries. |
| Sit in the bath. | Go to the post office. |
| Go for a run. | Go to the bank. |
| Go to a yoga class. | Volunteer at the school. |
| Shop with a friend. | Pay the bills. |
| Play a game. | Dust. |
| Ride a bike with my kids. | Buy a birthday present. |
| Hang out at the beach. | Get taxes pulled together. |
| Swim in the lake. | Pick kids up on time. |
| Get a manicure. | Call the exterminator. |

# TIME FLIES

Time is precious and fleeting. Time with your kids slips through your fingers. It's a cliché, but kids grow up too fast, and you don't want to wake up one day and realize that you missed their childhoods—so immersed and overwhelmed in car pools and other commitments that you neglected to savor the happy moments.

Time isn't something you can whip up in the kitchen, it's not something you can take to the bank, and it's not something people are willing to give to you.

Time is something you have to take. You must grab it. If you don't, lots can happen to take it from you. You can miss small things like those precious moments with your kids, the taste of really good food, or just enjoying life. Letting time slip can also have serious consequences. We were blown away when our MomsTown girlfriend Caroline told us this story:

One morning I was in the shower lathering up with my grapefruit shower gel like I always do when I noticed that my right breast was sensitive, and it wasn't just tenderness from PMS. It was a lump the size of a cherry pit. I got out and looked in the mirror but didn't see anything. Then I told my husband about it, and of course, his reaction was that I should schedule an appointment with my doctor as soon as possible. I nodded in agreement and naturally I was concerned, but I was also half an hour late for work. I quickly got dressed, headed to the office, and got so caught up in a project that before I knew it, I was late picking up the kids from school. Got them just in time, but then I didn't have anything in the fridge, so the kids and I ran to the supermarket to get dinner.

When we got home, it was almost 5 p.m., so I quickly got the kids settled with their homework and started making dinner. A load of un-folded laundry beckoned, so I folded that before getting everyone to the table. After dinner, more laundry, homework, and getting kids ready for bed. Exhausted, I headed for a quick shower. And then there I was again, grapefruit shower gel in hand, and I remembered the lump. At 9 p.m., it was too late to call the doctor, but I put it on tomorrow's mental to-do list. Tomorrow proved to be busier than the day before, and before I knew it, the weekend had arrived.

By Monday morning the breast didn't seem so sensitive and I had con-vinced myself it was nothing. I would just keep an eye on it myself. A week went by, a month, and then three months. I was so busy that I couldn't even squeeze in a call to the doctor's office to schedule the appointment. I was so busy that every time I thought about the lump, I rationalized that it was nothing. When I mentioned the lump to my sister, she looked at me like I was nuts, found my doctor's number in my BlackBerry, and persuaded me to pick up the phone.

The receptionist said the first appointment was six weeks away. That day arrived, nearly five months after taking that shower. There I was sitting in the doctor's office on one of those examining tables with the crinkly paper. I was naked except for a flimsy paper gown and sat perusing a month-old issue of People magazine when my doctor walked in. One look at her and I burst into tears. She asked me what was wrong, and I showed her the lump.

What came next was a total blur because it turns out the lump I'd brushed off was cancer. Yes, cancer! I'm happy to report the chemotherapy and radiation worked. I am one of the lucky ones. I am in full remission from cancer.

I'm also in full remission from being so wrapped up in the rest of the world that I forget about myself. I have a new appreciation about time and myself. The irony was that I was so busy doing everything so that everyone around me could have a great life that my own life could have easily slipped away.

Got tears in your eyes and an ache in your stomach? Us too. Caroline's story really makes you stop and think. Although it is an extreme example of a woman not taking care herself, it could happen to any of us. Easily! Remembering this story reminds us that not only does time fly, but time is precious. Time is yours to spend how you choose. Choose wisely.

# Chapter 4

# Frozen in Chaos

*H*ow do you feel every day when you wake up, you have so much to do you don't know where to start? You feel frozen. And we call it getting frozen in chaos. It happens when there's a huge stack of stress piled high on the kitchen counter or on the floor in the office. In that stack are due (and possibly overdue) bills, papers from the kids' schools, and unopened mail that needs to be purged. And it doesn't stop with the paper. You get mired in your closets, in the garage, frozen in your tracks in your kitchen, family room, and bedroom. It's easy to get overwhelmed by all the stuff in your busy life.

---

Don't agonize. Organize.          —*Florynce Kennedy*

---

What's a busy gal to do? We've tried cupping our hands around the corner of our eyes and singing "la, la, la, la," trying to avoid the mess.

But that doesn't work. Procrastinating and promising yourself you'll get to it later is also a bad plan. Having been frozen too many times, we decided enough already, let's start cutting the chaos.

---

Civilization begins with order, grows with liberty, and dies with chaos.

—*Will Durant*

---

Here are some of the e-mails we get from women who are overwhelmed by chaos in their homes, chaos in their cars, and chaos in their lives.

I can't keep track of appointments, bills, photos. Our home is a mess, my office is a mess, my van is a mess, and my life is a mess. Help! —Diane

Is my life in chaos? I watch Clean Sweep and I think, that is not just a couple of rooms in my house, this is my life. One ex-husband, one husband, four kids, one boxer, a mortgage, ballet, karate, PTA, and my full-time job. Although my life is full of wonderful people and things, I can't seem to find time to enjoy them. I'm always one step behind, including paying my bills, and it's starting to affect my credit rating! —Paula

Oh goodness! My home and life are out of control! We are always late to appointments or forgetting about them entirely. —Tricia

My own mother is even refusing to come over to our house unless it's an absolute emergency. It's that bad! —Alicia

I'm embarrassed about what it looks like and won't allow people into my home. Is it actually possible to get this place under
control? —Fran

Chaos is common. Chaos is a state of mind. Chaos is not being able
to see the countertops in your kitchen or the laundry room floor. Let's
face it. We all lead busy lives. When your kids are running around and
fighting, the phone is ringing, Susie needs to be picked up at soccer
practice, and you have no idea what's for dinner, you can feel the chaos
starting to get to you. Your nerves are shot, your temper is on edge, and
you feel like no matter what you do, you're not making any progress.

---

Organize your life around your dreams and
watch them come true.

—Anonymous

---

Happily, there are solutions. We have talked with enough organizing experts, friends, and frenzied women to learn what some of those
solutions are. First, however, try to bring down the level of frenzy.

# DO THE FENG SHUI SOFT-SHOE

Getting organized is not just about cleaning up the mess. According
to feng shui expert Terah Kathryn Collins, this is where people freeze. She
says, "People are starting at such a high level of chaos, their home is a disaster, the kids are running around, and they're short on time and patience." Truly getting organized is going to involve measuring, shopping,
and installing, which takes time, money, and consideration. Women
know that is what is involved and that's why they freeze in their steps.

Laugh, relax, and join us in making fun of FROZEN as an acronym:

**Frolic** in the chaos. This might sound crazy, but when you're frozen in chaos and not making progress, it's time to change your approach. Finding amusement in the mess improves your attitude. Approach the piles of laundry, papers, and dishes with a chuckle (even if there's nothing really funny about them). When you are able to find even the slightest humor in it, you'll approach the cleanup with more energy.

**Race** through the mess. Make a game or a sport out of the cleaning spree. Race to the smallest mess first. For example, if there is a short stack of papers on your nightstand, begin your race there. Once you've started racing through one mess, you'll find more energy to tackle the next. It's also important to note that racing works best in the open spaces. Don't even worry about the messes you can't see: the mess in the closets, cupboards, and under the bed. We have found the best way to cut chaos is to start with the messes that hit us when we first wake up, walk through the front door, or go into the kitchen to start dinner. Once the messes in the open spaces are cleaned up, it's time for the next step. Keep in mind a race could last a day, a week, even a month. It's a good idea to make a *race list*, a quick survey of the places where you'll be racing. Be sure to keep this list in a convenient place so you can check things off the list as you make progress.

**Open** drawers, closets, cupboards, and then open the trash bag. Start in the room where you spend most of your time. For many of us, it's the home office or the kitchen. Don't try to tackle every room at once. Focus on one room, one closet, or one cupboard at a time. Start purging and getting rid of the junk, the old papers, and the mess. Remember, one cupboard will probably only take about fifteen minutes to organize. If that's all the time there is in a day, then that's all that gets organized. At least it's one less cupboard of anxiety.

**Zen** it. Feel your stress melt away as you start to put the chaos behind you. This too is part of life, and all of life is meant to be enjoyed.

Honestly, the only reason we even believe in cutting the chaos is because it does bring peace of mind. We know from our own chaotic experience that when our lives feel out of control, we're not having as much fun. There's always something requiring our attention. Breathe deep, close your eyes, and picture how your life will be when the chaos is under control, when there is a feeling of Zen in your life and even in your closets.

**Edit** what you do. This is the reminder that you don't need to clean the entire house every day. Pick up a few toys, straighten the magazines and books, hang up a shirt or two, and call it a day.

**Note** it. Get a composition book to keep as a chaos journal. We've found that making notes to ourselves specifically about the chaotic points in our lives helps us to see them more clearly. It also helps us to see how truly manageable they really are. Once you start doing this, chaos loses its control over you and you start controlling the chaos.

## CULPRITS OF CHAOS

Now that we have started to change your attitudes about the mess in your life, let's start to deal with it by asking you a few questions:

1. Who is causing the chaos in your life? The most logical culprits are always the kids (and we have several ideas to get them organized). But are there others? Husband? People at work? Heaven forbid: could Mom be the problem?
2. Is this more of a time problem than an organizing problem?
3. Is this a storage issue? Are you pinched for space in your living quarters and fresh out of places to put things? Maybe it is time to consider some storage bins in the closets or even a small shed in the backyard to hold the overflow.

4. Is this a pack rat problem? Are you or your husband trying to hold on to too much stuff in all the corners? Do the kids have more toys out than they can possibly enjoy at one time? Time to stash that stuff in a convenient cubbyhole until you really want it.

5. Do you really need help? Is this a situation where a housekeeper or a babysitter could give you a few hours of sanity to restore order?

6. Are you a perfectionist? No family situation is ever going to be neat as a pin with every little thing in its place. Life is messy. Decide upon the level of chaos you can tolerate, and find happiness in hitting the tolerance zone most days.

After you've asked yourself those questions and made a brief self-evaluation, take a closer look at the chaotic culprits in your life:

1. The kids. This is a tough one because as their mother you want to take care of them. You find yourself picking up after them and making their beds (even when they're old enough to do it themselves) because, quite frankly, it's easier, faster, and you're *picking your battles*. The problem with this approach is that you're setting yourself up for years of chaotic discord. You're also training them that you'll always (or someone will always) be there to pick up after them. (Maybe this is what happened to our husbands!)

2. The husband. Here's a truth about our significant others. Some of us have been blessed with husbands that are tidy. They pick up after themselves (and sometimes even pick up after us). And some of us are blessed with guys who couldn't find the hamper if it were clothespinned to their butts. This is another toughie. With the guy who's not into picking up after himself and you stop doing it for him, you run the risk that he won't even notice, and you'll just aggravate yourself more.

A friend of ours put her husband's clothes and shoes under his pillow. She says it only took a couple of nights for him to get the point. Now it's kind of a running joke between them, but he's helping out (most of the time). Another friend hides her husband's stuff. When he is looking for his toothbrush or shaving cream, she just responds, "Gosh, honey, I don't know where it went." This is one of our favorites, even if it's a bit passive aggressive. We also find it's helpful to simply ask for help.

# NEED A LITTLE PROFESSIONAL HELP?

When we need organizing reinforcements, we believe in turning to the top. Julie Morgenstern is one of the best in her field. She has written numerous books to help us busy people bring order and peace to our world. We asked her what problems women most often run up against when they're trying to get organized. She told us, "Women get overwhelmed thinking they have to organize everything at once."

To avoid being overwhelmed, Julie advises:

⊚ Start in one room. Choose the room you spend the most time in and start there. The most common starting points are the kitchen, bathroom, or bedroom.

⊚ Organize that one room completely before moving on to another room.

⊚ Get a box or container and mark it "Belongs Elsewhere." When you're organizing a room and you have things that belong in other places (other than in that room), toss them in the box. Don't try to take them elsewhere. When you do, you get caught up in zigzag organizing. You get sidetracked and start moving from room to room, never finishing any of them.

Before you get started, use her three steps to making the job of getting organized a whole lot easier and a whole lot quicker:

1. *Analyze.* Sit down for an hour and analyze the space you want to organize. Focus on what is working and what is not.
2. *Strategize.* Plan what tools and containers you will need to accomplish your goal. Get out a tape measure and do the necessary measuring. You should also plan what the space will look like when you're finished.
3. *Attack.* Go after it. Start tossing, moving, rearranging, and organizing.

## JULIE'S BONUS TIP

Everyone has places where piles tend to build. For example, homework on the kitchen counter, shoes and backpacks by the back door, miscellaneous items on a table by the front door, bills near the phone, and paperwork on the nightstand. These things are landing there because that's where the work is done. Create an organized space at that location. For example, if your kids do homework in the kitchen, move some unused pots or bowls and create an organized homework station in a kitchen cupboard. It's far too much effort to stow things in places other than where they are used. Remember, getting organized should not force you to change habits; it should work around your flow and everyday life.

\* \* \*

Ultimately, you create much of the chaos you let into your life. You're the one who agrees to volunteer on too many committees, you're the one who takes on extra work at the office, and you're the one who lets things pile up around you. But as we've mentioned, it doesn't have to be this way, and we have a few more strategies we'd like to share with you.

# THE CONTROL PANEL

We never see the captain come down the aisle of an airplane looking for the switch he needs to lower the landing gear. Can you imagine flying over Albuquerque and hearing the pilot over the loudspeaker ask if anyone has seen that little red button? Of course not! We're being goofy, but the point is this: it's all at his fingertips.

So why is it when you're paying bills, scheduling appointments, or doing your office work, you don't have everything you need at your fingertips? We learned this great tip from a gal we would describe as a woman who gets things done. She is one of the most productive women we've ever met in our entire lives. She is an accountability coach. Who even knew that was a job?

## A MomsTown Tip
### ON CONTROLLING CHAOS

> I'm an entrepreneur. Time is money. I schedule a certain amount of time to make that money. Every keystroke and movement I make has to be at my fingertips. When I sit down at my desk to work, I can't afford to keep getting out of my chair.
>
> I also travel a lot in my work. On a trip home from the East Coast I was leaving the plane when the captain stepped out to thank us for choosing his airline. The door to the cockpit was open. I looked inside and it dawned on me he has everything he needs to fly this huge jet right at his fingertips. His job is to sit down and fly this huge jet. He's responsible for hundreds of lives. He needs to have his environment as streamlined as possible so he can focus on the task at hand. That's when it hit me. I need a Control Panel! That evening I stayed up until two in the morning reorganizing my office, making it my cockpit! —Anne

You might not be flying a 747, but you are probably flying too much by the seat of your pants. To get control you need to establish areas that are streamlined and organized and enable you to be efficient.

You need Control Panels in the laundry room, closets, bathrooms, and office.

For example, in the **laundry room**, the detergent and softener should be within reaching distance of the washing machine, not tucked away where they're hard to reach. There should also be a trash bin in the laundry room for lint, tags, strings, and rocks that fall out of the kids' pockets. It's also a great idea to have a container to toss loose change into. We always find quarters, nickels, and, if we're lucky, dollar bills in the dryer. This could be the start of a college education fund.

Organization in the **closet** is really important. Think about it. You start every day digging in your closet. Your morning closet experience can set your mood for the day. If you're packing a gym bag for after work and can't find a sports bra in the mound of clothing on the shelf, you get frustrated. Suddenly, a disorganized pile of clothing turns into a little voice in your head screaming, "I'm fat and now I can't work out." There needs to be a system in the closet. Just as in the laundry room, the most-used items should be accessible.

## Closet Quickies

- Put out-of-season clothes away.
- Take fifteen minutes to clean one dresser drawer at a time. You don't have to clean them all at once.
- Pack old and unused shoes in a box and mark them for donation.
- Set aside all items that need to be tailored or repaired, then put them in the car. (Things never get fixed or hemmed when they're hanging in the closet.)
- Organize the jewelry box.
- Put similar clothing in sections—jeans in one area, sweaters in another, and so on.

In the **bathroom** the Control Panel is at the sink, under the sink, and in the linen closet. At the sink, clear as much as possible from the counter top, including toothbrush holders, brushes, hair dryers, moisturizers, and makeup.

## Bathroom Quickies

- ⊚ Get separate trays for brushes, combs, scrunchies, clips, and headbands, and put these trays or baskets in drawers and cupboards. For example, hair spray, mousse, and other hair products are in one basket under the sink. Mouthwash, floss, and whiteners are in another. We even put plastic stadium shelving under the sink to make it easier to see what's at the back of the cupboard.
- ⊚ Straighten out the linen closet. It's amazing how towels have a way of tangling themselves.
- ⊚ Have a space designated for extra stock. This includes toilet paper, tissues, toothbrushes, and toothpaste. That way it's easy to know when you're running out of something: you can just take a quick glancing inventory of the designated space.
- ⊚ Toss out old polish, old nail files, old makeup, and dinosaurs. A dinosaur is the eighth of an inch of moisturizer that's left in the bottom of the pump bottle and that you can't get out but feel wasteful tossing (in fact, you've already started using the replacement).

In your **office** think of the desk as your Control Panel. Everything should be within the reach and spin of your chair. You should be able to reach envelopes, stamps, phone/fax, computer, printer, current files, pens, stapler, and other office supplies without leaving your chair. This is may not benefit your bottom, but it does benefit the bottom line when it comes to getting a handle on the paperwork.

# OUR ROBOTIC PERSONAL ASSISTANT

You may not be aware of it, but there is a genie in that computer in your house. If Dad and the kids have taken charge of it, they are depriving Mom of one of her potentially most powerful tools against the forces of chaos. For example, there are now dozens of computer programs, such as MS Outlook, Sidekick, or Daytimer, that are designed to help you keep track of your tasks; your to-do list; addresses and phone numbers; daily, weekly, monthly, or even yearly planning; reminders for important dates; and many other items to bring order to your life. These programs also allow you to print out daily to-do lists or shopping lists. Or, if you are really into technology, you can synchronize all of your information on a handheld PDA and slip it into your purse.

There are also home finance programs such as Quicken or MS Money that help you to keep track of all the bills; provide online credit card balances and bank accounts; and generally allow you to automate your family finances.

Cooking? There are amazing websites, such as foodnetwork.com or epicurious.com, that provide recipes and shopping lists and nutritional advice for all sorts of meals.

Family photos? Take a look at the albums and online sharing services that make photo organization a cinch in places such as Picasa 2 or Shutterfly.

If you have not done so already, put that genie to work and enjoy the organization it brings into your life—not to mention the extra time.

In the **kitchen** we have developed a Control Panel to put an end to all the running we've been doing. Isn't it funny that when you're making breakfast, packing lunches, or making dinner in the evening, you wish you had a pair of skates? It's to the pantry, back to the fridge, to the Tupperware cupboard, to the dishwasher, to the stove, back to the sink.

If you can organize your kitchen, you can
organize your life.

—*Louis Parrish*

Cross-kitchen cooking is not an Olympic event. We don't mind burning a few extra calories, but cross-kitchen cooking is more irritating than slimming. Why are you running a marathon to make a meal? To streamline your cupboards and make your time in the kitchen more enjoyable, use the Control Panel philosophy. Keep the most-used items within reach.

For example, we're always using the sandwich bags to pack lunches, but we keep the bags in the pantry. It makes more sense to take the bags out of the pantry and keep them closer to the area where we pack the lunches. Sometimes we're so close to our routine, we fail to see any other way.

## PREPARE FOR A UFO SIGHTING

We hope that many of these suggestions are helpful and that many even may be old tricks of which you simply needed to be reminded. On the other hand, if this is all coming as news to you, you might consider a UFO sighting. What's a UFO?

**Un-**
**Familiar**
**Observer**

This is a way of "sighting" a room. It's pretending as though you are walking into a room for the first time, especially if you've lived in the same house for years. It's a fresh perspective. It's looking at your floor plan, your furniture, and your routines to recognize patterns. When you get too close to your mess, you can't even see it, let alone fix it. This is why people love to hire an organizer. Organizers are unfamiliar observers. It's all new to them. They're not emotionally attached to the stuff, the space, or the setting.

Nice, if you can afford it. However, you can be your own UFO or you can invite a sister, a friend, or a neighbor to do the sighting for you. Fresh eyes will see things you overlook. It's nothing to be ashamed of or to feel stupid about. After you've had a sighting, you'll think, "Why didn't I think of that?" or to put it in Wendy's words, "Why didn't I move my oven mitts closer to the oven a long time ago?" She explains, "I've always kept them in the drawer by the stove. But I never use them for the stove; I need them for the oven. I guess that's why they're called *oven mitts*, duh!"

\* \* \*

UFOs are liberating. And so is cutting chaos from your life. We know we've put a lot of different strategies in this chapter. Hopefully, you'll find one or perhaps all of them useful. We know that every time we get a new tip, it reminds us we need to keep moving and to not get frozen in our tracks.

The good news is that all the tasks we've just discussed only have to be done once or twice a year. You won't have to create a Control Panel in the laundry room every week. Once it's done, you can maintain it with much less effort.

We would never recommend carving out an entire Saturday or weekend to overhaul the entire house, unless that worked best for you. We have come to learn from most of the women in our lives that we get more accomplished when we are consistent and take on projects one at a time.

We're also always happier and life moves along more easily when we're fluid, not frozen.

# Resources for Organization
## BOOKS
Checklists for Life: 104 Lists to Help You Get Organized by Kirsten Lagatree (Random House, 1999).

The Big Clean: How to Organize Your Pad and Free Your Mind by Kim Rinehart (Bright Yellow Hat, 2004).

Ready, Set, Organize! A Workbook for the Organizationally Challenged by Pipi Campbell Peterson and Mary Campbell (Jist Publishing, 1998).

Organizing from the Inside Out by Julie Morgenstern (Henry Holt, 1998).

Organizing Plain and Simple by Donna Smallin (Storey Publishing, 2002).

It's All Too Much: An Easy Plan for Living a Richer Life with Less Stuff by Peter Walsh (Free Press, 2006).

## WEBSITES
www.onlineorganizing.com

www.creativehomemaking.com

www.ataglance.com

www.solutionscatalog.com

www.franklincovey.com

www.organizedhome.com

www.myorganizedlife.com

*Chapter 5*

# A River Runs
# Through It

$\mathcal{T}$he big thaw is on in your house. The glacier you were stuck on in a sea of arctic chaos is now beginning to melt. Your organizational skills are beginning to stream and you are ready for the next step. It's a technique we have developed to bring order out of chaos, and it is named for one of our favorite novellas by Norman Maclean. Written in 1976, it was made into a beautiful movie by Robert Redford. (Of course, it didn't hurt that Brad Pitt starred in it.)

We like to call this organizational journey A River Runs Through It, because a river changes organically every day, as does your domestic life. A river also changes over time. The course changes; the obstacles in the river change. Your life is in constant fluid motion. When you approach getting organized with fluid thought you are in a better mental space to handle the tasks at hand. The simple visualization of a river or a babbling brook brings about a peaceful calm that is necessary when approaching any project. It's also not a bad way to approach your life.

# THE OCI SYNDROME

We also came up with the flowing river concept because we needed to find a way to handle our OCI syndrome. The other day we were laughing on the phone with a friend of ours, Terah Kathryn Collins. She is the founder of the Western School of Feng Shui and the author of several books on the subject of feng shui.

She says that when she's working with clients, she recognizes three emotional leads that alert women that it's time to clean out. She finds that the clients are

**O**verwhelmed
**C**onfused
**I**rritated

Well, let us tell you, when she told us that, we both burst out laughing. Immediately, we saw the acronym as the disorder in our busy mom lives, and at that very moment, we exhibited all three traits. The laughter helped us. If you ever doubted that attitude and fun will make a difference in getting organized, reread "Frozen in Chaos" and doubt no longer. After we both agreed and laughed about the fact that we were so OCI, we decided to clean the office.

---

*Feng Shui* literally means wind-water. It is the Chinese geomantic practice in which a structure or site is chosen or configured so as to harmonize with the spiritual forces that inhabit it.

—*Merriam-Webster Online*

---

We met a woman named Amy who also suffered from OCI. Amy felt as though her life was spinning out of control and that her house was in utter chaos.

Quite honestly, she was right. Some friends asked us if we wouldn't mind dropping in on Amy to give her a helping hand. We did, and the moment she opened the door with a baby on her hip, she broke into tears. Amy needed help. She needed someone who understood how she was feeling. We're moms and we understand how overwhelming life can be some days.

Her emotions were high because she was in need of a helping hand: her nose was barely above the waterline. Amy had stuff every-where.

Being a great sport, Amy took us on a roaring rapids ride through her house. At every bend of her house, we encountered a class-five rapid. As anyone who has ever been river rafting knows, a class-five rapid will definitely send you swimming for the shore (that is if you survive the whitewater). There were boxes, clothes, toys, papers, and stuff every-where. Every countertop was cluttered. In her bathroom, the counter was covered with toothbrushes, toothpaste, hair spray, makeup, brushes, towels, and a razor.

In her kitchen we couldn't even see the countertops, and we were sure there was a refrigerator somewhere. Oh, there it was—covered in artwork, calendars, paperwork, and magnets. We needed to fetch a lad-der to get all the stuff off the top of the fridge.

The family room was in the same disorder. There were boulders and dams scattered throughout. The family had no place to relax, and even if they found a quiet shore, getting to it meant oars in the water for a hard paddle.

**Just as a river gathers debris and carries it downstream, we gather stuff all day long and carry it with us.**

Amy, like so many of the women we talk to every week, felt swamped by so much stuff and didn't know where to start. Our answer for Amy and for you is simple. Start charting. Chart how the river flows in your home.

## River Rule #1:
### LET FLOW BE YOUR GUIDE

To chart your river, begin at the headwaters. This is where the river trip begins. For example, if you choose to use the front door as the head-waters, chart the direction the water flows when it enters your home. Try it. Go to your front door, and when you walk in, ask yourself, "Where does the energy go? What is the most common path people take when entering my home?" This is also the path of the river. Follow that path and remove any obstacles that disrupt the flow. There could be a table or an ottoman that you walk around every day and never notice how it blocks the river's path.

## River Rule #2:
### REMOVE ALL BOULDERS

Boulders are fixed objects in the river. They are big, they are in the way, and they are going to take a little muscle to move. Boulders are those formidable items that have been placed in the pathway. You may not even notice some boulders because you've grown accustomed to navigating around them. Boulders may be tables, chairs, sofas, settees, armoires, dressers, floor lamps, or bookcases. They can even be the bed you sleep in every night. Now, we're not going to ask you to sleep on the floor, but boulders need to be moved to a place where they don't disrupt the flow.

## River Rule #3:
### ESCAPE THE EDDIES

Now that you've encountered your first boulders, let the flow carry you downriver. Continuing to follow the flow throughout your home, you come across the first eddy. Eddies are swirling pools of water. It's hard to get out of an eddy. In our homes eddies are the dumping sites where mail, purses, keys, backpacks, and other miscellaneous items pile up. When debris gets caught in an eddy, the only way to get it out is to physically pull it out. Items do not escape eddies on their own.

## River Rule #4:
### BAN THE DAMS

Every home has a dam. This is the area where the flow comes to a complete stop. The boulders we mentioned in River Rule #2 may disrupt the flow, but the dam stops it. A dam is a place where clutter is allowed to build up and you end up flooded in chaos. That flood of clutter starts to spill over into other areas of your life.

For example, Cary is a friend of ours who has a fabulous walk-in closet. There's plenty of space in the closet, but you'd never know it. There were clothes piled on the floor, boxes of pictures stacked high, and racks of shoes (most of which she hasn't worn in years). She complains that she never has anything to wear. The truth is she can't find anything to wear.

Cary starts every day confronting a dam. Her energy gets bottled up from the moment she steps out of the shower and tries to find an outfit. This energy blocker is causing her a great deal of unnecessary stress. We recommended to Cary that her river trip should begin when she first wakes up. The moment her feet touch the floor is when her journey begins. Clearing a path through her closet to the shower—even just to her sink area where she stores her toiletries—will help her to get the energy flowing.

> I did it. I cleaned my closet. I've been meaning to do it for two years, but I kept finding ways out of doing it. I had all kinds of excuses. I never really recognized that my closet was disrupting my entire day. I can't tell you how great it is to wake up and go into a clean closet. I actually found a pair of pants that still had the tags on. Damn, that felt good. —Cary

## River Rule #5:
### ALLOW THE TRIP TO TAKE ITS OWN TIME

Now continue to follow the flow. Follow it into the family room, living room, bedroom, closets, kids' rooms, and so on, removing boulders along the way. This flowing approach to organization automatically instills a sense of calm. You'll feel better recognizing there is a flow to your home. Remove boulders fifteen minutes at a time. No need to ride all the rapids in one day. A good river trip takes its time.

Also keep in mind there are rivers everywhere. There's a river in the garage, in the yard, and there's even a river you navigate once you back out of your driveway. Consider the paths you take every day to be river trips.

For example, when Heather drives to work every day, she knows there is a more direct and quicker route than the one she takes. That quick drive, however, takes her past several busy intersections, through half a dozen street lights, past a busy high school, and even through a roundabout. Instead, she opts to take a path that extends her drive by about five minutes (at the most), but it's a much prettier and calmer path.

Her route takes a big sweeping curve that puts her on a road along the ocean. The drive puts her in a better mood; it gives her a sense of calm every time she rounds the turn. This trip to her place of work helps her set the tone for how her day is going to flow. Consider the rivers you're navigating on a daily basis. If your daily drive has you gripping the steering wheel, then try mapping a different course.

The purpose of A River Runs Through It is to highlight the impact your environment has on your state of well-being. Bringing nature (even in theory) into the house helps restore harmony to your busy life.

## Environmental Tips on Clutter

1. Clutter matters. Clutter is a state of congestion. It's like having a head cold. When you're all stuffed up, you operate at a diminished energy level. Start decongesting your home by first agreeing that clutter is stagnating.

2. Clutter is simply homeless possessions. It's stuff with no place to go—mail on the nightstand, homework on the kitchen counter, shoes in the foyer. Give those possessions a home and you'll start making huge strokes in the world of organizing.

3. Say no to new clutter. Let go of old possessions before allowing new possessions to enter the home. If you buy a new pair of pants, donate an old pair. If you expect lots of toys at an upcoming birthday party, then get your kids to pitch in and gather up old toys to donate or toss.

It's important to remember, however, that not every day has to be completely cleaned up. Not every day is going to be an easy float down the river. There will be days that feel as though you've completely tumbled over a waterfall and landed in a pool of disaster. The key to surviving is after you've been able to reach the surface, catch your breath and start treading water, look around, and realize that it's sink or swim. (In other words, do something!)

When you decide to swim, then getting organized is really all about style. You can spread your wings and butterfly, freestyle, or backstroke into it. No particular style is right or wrong. It truly comes down to what works best for you and your family.

To further guide you on the river in your home, we've drafted a one-week river trip itinerary. On a real river trip you get in and out of the river, you ride the rapids, and it's so much fun, you'll start looking for a bigger river with more challenges, more whitewater. That said, go in with your head, not your heart. We're trying to get something done here, ladies. Don't sit and ooh and ahh over memorabilia. You'll have more time for that later, once things are organized. Organizing, like a river trip, requires common sense. Be practical, and don't get in over your head. Don't get so excited that you try to conquer the entire river in a day.

## SEVEN DAYS ON THE RIVER

**Day 1:** Assess how much time you have in the day for the river trip. Is it fifteen minutes or two hours? And are you in the raft by yourself or do you have a co-captain? Schedule the time in your organizer or on the calendar. Making a river trip appointment with yourself is another way to assure that it will get started.

**Day 2:** Choose your point of entry. Is it your front door? Is it the master closet? Is it the Tupperware drawer in the kitchen? Where do you want your river trip to begin? It's up to you; you're the guide. Survey the area.

**Day 3:** Decide who is going along with you. You don't want to navigate the rapids on your own. Not only is it smart to have someone with you, it's also a lot more fun. Decide who is going to be responsible for what.

**Day 4:** Go shopping. This is the best part of traveling. But don't forget the list. It's amazing how quickly containers, baskets, shelves, and drawer dividers can add up. You definitely don't want to overbuy, because then you'll just have more stuff. And stuff slows you down on the water.

**Day 5:** Open the floodgates, clear the dam, and start bailing. Get a trash bag and a donation bin and start getting rid of all the old stuff. Remember, this is in just one area. Keep your focus on one segment of the river at a time.

**Day 6:** Install and replenish. This is the day to install the containers and organizers you've purchased and give all the remaining stuff a home.

**Day 7:** Take a much deserved breather. You've earned it! Get rested, there's another stretch of river calling your name.

## Resources

Western School of Feng Shui, www.wsfs.com

International Feng Shui Guild,
    www.InternationalFengShuiGuild.org

American Society of Interior Designers, www.asid.org

National Association of Professional Organizers, www.napo.net

The Western Guide to Feng Shui: Creating Balance, Harmony, and Prosperity in
    Your Environment by Terah Kathryn Collins (Hay House, 1996)

# Chapter 6

# Man Math, Lady Luck, and Money Talks

*W*e recently asked the women on our MomsTown forum, "What would you do with an extra $1,000 a month?" Much to our surprise, they had to think about it, and even more to our surprise, not one mom asked if she could have more than $1,000.

We talk to women every day who are wishy-washy on the subject of money. For some reason, women have trouble discussing dollars. They get tongue-tied when it comes to admitting that money is important and that, by golly, we want more of it. Here's a little something we've learned: if you want something, speak up.

When you go to a restaurant and want to order something to eat, you have to choose a meal from the menu. If you left it up to the waiter, he'd bring you a basket of bread and water until you decided. And that's why most of us are living on a bread and water budget.

**It's time to order from the Money Menu.**

It's time to tell yourself how much money you really want. Write it down. Make it real, not just imaginary millions. How much monthly, how much annually, and how much for retirement? Most of us haven't given it much thought. We are just *uncomfortably comfortable*.

Being uncomfortably comfortable doesn't mean you're financially set by any means. We're talking about the kind of comfort zone that makes us resistant to change. It's why we stay in jobs we don't like. We're too afraid to quit, and the current path is familiar. It's why we talk about finding ways to make money from home but never do it. We would have to step out of our comfort zone, take risks, and ask for what we want. This makes us uncomfortable. It's much easier for us to stay put, cut out discount coupons, and continue paying the minimum amount on our credit cards.

Everyone we communicate with on a daily basis has some kind of money issue. More often than not the issue is this: money goes out a heck of a lot faster than it comes in. Even though most families have dual incomes, money is still tight. Where we used to live paycheck to paycheck, we now live paychecks to paychecks. The fact that you have two separate checks coming in hasn't changed the fact that you are still just eking it out.

> My husband got a raise but it still doesn't feel like any extra money. We have more coming in but it still just goes out. We are trying to pay off as much of our debt as possible but it seems as though there's no end in sight. —Carly

Let's face it, coupons and credit card minimums alone don't cut it. When you take this route, you never get ahead. At this point you have two choices. One is to continue to spend more time doing what you've always done. The other is to do something about it. Here is a money insight to contemplate: you are as wealthy as you think.

# WHY MONEY IS IMPORTANT

It buys the necessities—food, shelter, water, clothing, electricity, and health care.

It buys freedom.

It buys time.

It buys peace of mind.

It buys vacations.

It buys gifts.

It buys a visit from the tooth fairy.

It buys date night.

It buys cars.

It buys plane tickets.

It buys surprises.

It buys reunions with friends and loved ones.

It buys time off from work.

Money is actually a positive indication of your standard of living. It can give you control over your lifestyle. Even if you have no desire to live like Trump, you can live the life to which you aspire, and that life starts with your attitude about money.

Money is a complex symbol. It can make you happy and it can send you into a complete panic. And the funny thing is that it's just a piece of paper. What is its inherent value? A dollar can now buy us a third of a cup of coffee. But seriously, it's wreaking havoc on our lives and our relationships, and it shouldn't.

# MAN MATH AND LADY LUCK

That relationship havoc can be avoided by relating to each other from a place of understanding, an understanding that men and women can be fundamentally different when it comes to how they look at and feel about money. We call those different approaches and attitudes Man

Math and Lady Luck. Neither one is negative; they're just different. Often, money fights will start because one or both parties reject the other person's approach to saving or spending money because they see it as foolish, uninformed, irresponsible, or too conservative. Let's take a look at our theory of Man Math and Lady Luck.

## MAN MATH

When men address money issues, they immediately jump into fix-it mode. Their initial step is to mentally calculate how much the bills add up to each month—they conclude the monthly deposits cover it all.

Of course, rarely does any one month of expenses mirror a prior month. There are always extra expenses—car repairs, children's doctor appointments, new glasses, new winter clothing, holiday gifts. These are expenses that go over and above the income coming in for the month. In most households there is a fixed amount to use for living expenses. With that said, husbands remember all of the deposits, yet they have conveniently forgotten all the debits.

That's Man Math. Not to mention the way men can matter-of-factly be so certain of "the facts." How is it they can twist money reality and then be so black and white about it? For example they are convinced that we, as women, should be able to manage all the household finances, to pay the bills, and to pay off the credit cards—no matter how much is in the checking account. It is as if men think we can make money magically appear. Because, for some reason, they think it magically disappears.

> Every month I tell my husband I need to pull from our savings to cover our expenses. Every month he asks me, "Where did all the money go?" Every month I show him the list of bills. We repeat this month after month. It's no longer a magic show, it's a comedy routine. —Eve

We're not here to harp on the guys, because as women we, too, have a unique approach to money. Men often do look at money more mathematically than women. And, women have a way of becoming more emotional about it, especially when our men stop short of accusing us of being irresponsible with the family dollars. Here is a case in point from a post on our MomsTown message board:

> Darling Husband: I make $X every month. We should be able
>    to live off of that. I need to see a list of all the bills.
> Me: (making a mental rundown, off the top of my head) We
>    have about $200 left for food.
> DH: That can't be. You need to start shopping at cheaper stores.
> Me: Hell no. You need to stop expecting steak every night!
> DH: You need to go back to work!
> Me: And who is going to watch our kids?

While we recognize that men have a peculiar way of deducing the ending balance of household finances, we have to admit that women have a few of their own unique twists. Women may not be so innocent when the Money Talk leads to the Money Fight. In truth, most of us can share part of the blame with our role as Lady Luck.

## LADY LUCK

Women have a gift. Even if we are looking at the dwindling supply of cash on a weekly basis, we insist upon taking an optimistic view. We somehow think that it will all work out and that there will be enough money to go around, even when we are staring at evidence to the contrary. It is the Lady Luck syndrome, and we are all positively guilty. So what is Lady Luck all about? Lady Luck means looking at money from an emotional place. When we say "emotional," we mean good emotions and challenging emotions. Good emotions express an optimistic faith in the creation of more money. You believe more money can and will come in—even if you're not immediately sure where that money source might be.

Why do women believe this? We believe this because we create. If we can create life, we can certainly create more money.

Now, we can't say all men exhibit Man Math or that all women are Lady Luck, but by and large this is our experience. We hosted many Big Break parties. The theme of the parties was to inspire business creativity, create a network, and offer tips and resources. Women would laugh and raise their hands when we asked, "Has anyone had the Money Talk from their husband?" All the wives knew, without an explanation, what we meant. This is what happens when Man Math talks cash. Wives are immediately put on the defensive with questions such as "Where did all the money go?" "What did you spend it all on?" You get the picture. When he starts questioning the way you spend money, you start defending the reasons why the money seems to go out faster than it comes in.

It doesn't matter if you're a stay-at-home mom or a working mom, you end up in this defensive role because typically you're the one spending the money. You're the one writing the checks for all the bills. You don't want to have to explain every purchase down to why you buy organic foods or why Johnny needed new clothes and shoes when he grew two inches over the summer. You start defending why you spent so much on gas, and why the kids have not learned how to turn the lights off when they leave a room. All of a sudden, he's saying that you don't know how to teach your kids the value of the dollar, and apparently, in his eyes, you don't know the value of the dollar either.

Then he forges into his I'm-here-to-save-the-day, Man Math mode, "I must see all the bills for the last twelve months!" After he scrutinizes your work with great fanfare, in a gruff voice he concludes, "Hmmmf, well, we need more money. So, when are you going to be able to contribute more to the family?" Needless to say, neither the arithmetic shenanigans of Man Math nor the defensive arguments of Lady Luck are going to help the bottom line.

We have some tips on how to bring in more money, which we will address in the "Career" and "Big Break" chapters, but for now let's deal with the Money Fight.

# HOW WE TALK ABOUT MONEY

When we started a conversation about money on our radio show and posted messages about money in our MomsTown forum, women came out of the cul-de-sac. It turns out women are more interested in money than anyone thought. Magazine editors would have us think that we all want more sex. The reality is that we all want more money, and when women start talking about it, we discover that we have a lot in common.

## MONEY REALITY

I'm no longer afraid to admit I want more money because the truth is I need it. My son is diabetic and his medication costs hundreds of dollars every month. Money is a lifesaver in our family. —Lisa

We have two student loans and too many credit cards. We need money just to keep our nostrils above the waterline. —Kelly

My husband is in the military and we have two small kids. I've already sold everything we don't need on eBay and I still don't have enough to make the bills. —Barb

My husband and I both work full-time and I want to cut back on my hours or work out some flex time to spend more time with my kids. But we can't afford the cut in pay. —Anne

At this rate, neither I nor my husband will be able to retire at the

*age of sixty-five. We have no savings and I'm sure we'll be working
into our seventies and that's depressing. It takes money to retire.*
—Robin

MomsTown moms have come to realize that we all want three
things when it comes to money:

1. We want to feel better about it.
2. We want more of it and don't want to feel guilty
   about that.
3. We want to be able to talk about it without
   fighting about it.

Let's examine that last item. It's one thing to recognize that you
want more money and that money is an issue in your marriage. The
greatest deterrent from getting more money is the way we think and
talk about it. Because in households across America, we're not talking
about money, we're fighting about money. Call it a discussion or a squab-
ble, but according to *Money* magazine (March 2006), seven in ten couples admit to fighting over money.

We think the other three couples in the poll are either newlyweds
or lying.

## THE MONEY FIGHT

We have noticed that when we talk to our girlfriends about money, the
conversation gets a bit uncomfortable. We'll admit to having discussions or disagreements, but few of us really want to admit that we fight
over money.

Our friend Heike sent us this e-mail describing how her money
fight usually starts. We want to share it with you because it sounds all
too familiar:

Our money fight usually starts like this, something innocent:

> Husband: I saw the credit card bill today. Do we REALLY owe
> $X? How can that be?
> Wife: Do you remember paying $X for the car repairs last
> week? Where do you think that money came from?
> Husband: I NEED TO SEE ALL THE BILLS! WHAT ELSE DO
> WE OWE?
>
> —Heike

It's the classic Money Fight between husband and wife. It goes from the Money Talk to the Money Grudge, followed by Money Tears, and hopefully the Money Makeup. (If you miss this last step, you're probably in the midst of the Money Divorce.)

During a recent girls' night out, Kelly arrived after drinks were served. She had the look; we knew something unpleasant had delayed her. She sat down and blurted out, "I just had the Money Talk." We all groaned. It was truly a *Sex-in-the-City*-for-married-women moment. We ordered her a double and she began to spill. She says she was midstride out the door when her husband asked her about the credit card bill left on the kitchen table. He wanted to know why she had charged the groceries. Still in midstride she answered, "Because I never have any cash on me, and I was in a hurry." She says the conversation went downhill from there, and that's why she was late.

* * *

If money wasn't so important, we wouldn't be talking about it and we certainly wouldn't be fighting over it. But wouldn't you know, it's one of the leading causes of divorce. In fact, married couples are not the only ones fighting over money. Nations, religions, and cultures fight over money. And if there was life on another planet, they'd probably be fighting over it too! It also doesn't matter how much income is brought into a household. What matters is how much is going out. The fights are not about what comes in; they are about what goes out and who escorts it out the door.

During the Money Talk, where do we make the critical error so it turns from talking to fighting? We've had enough Money Talks in our lives and talked with enough women about their experiences as well to know how the Money Talk goes south.

You know the Money Talk is headed in the wrong direction when you see the DEBIT red flag.

## DEBIT

**Defend:** You become defensive when your husband asks questions regarding money.

**Exaggerate:** When words like "always" and "never" and "all" get tossed around.

**Blame:** "You, you, you . . ." "What did *you* spend the money on?" "What did *you* do with all the money?" "Why didn't *you* pay off the credit card?"

**Intimidate:** "I need to see all the bills." This is when one person in the Money Talk tries to become the Money Hero riding in to fix the mess.

**Time:** Timing is critical. If it's the wrong time, you can forget about talking because you will be fighting.

We try to never have the Money Talk at these times:

Late at night

When one or both of us are tired

When we've just received bad news (Conversely, when we've just received good news, that's a better time to talk money. In fact, right after sex is not a bad time either.)

When one or both of us are in a rush

When the kids are present

When the first bills after the holidays arrive

If you stop and look at it rationally (married couples rarely do), there are a number of ways to ward off the Money Fights and work together for a better family financial picture. Here's a good start:

## 1. Keep each other in the loop of the finances.

In the money game, it is best if you function as a team. Typically, we marry someone who has a different money mood than we do. Perhaps we're the saver and he treats shopping at Home Depot or the food warehouse as a weekend sporting event. Or he's counting the pennies and you're hiding the shopping bags in the trunk of the car until he goes to work. Even if your differences are not that extreme, both of you have to be kept in the loop about the reality of your finances.

*Step one:* Acknowledge and admit your money mood. Do either of the scenarios fit one or both of you? Neither of you is likely to change your behavior much, though the second step will help you work together and think before you swipe.

*Step two:* Have a money meeting to set savings goals and debt reduction goals. Carve out the time to discuss where you stand today and where you want to be in one month, one year, and in the long term. Planning together is the key.

## 2. Share the bottom line no matter how painful it is.

Once the truth of a financial situation is discussed, a solution can be applied. To keep an open dialogue about money issues, first pick a good time, and then keep the emotion out of it. Just the facts, ma'am.

## 3. Agree on a time, weekly or monthly, to discuss financial affairs.

Now that you both have agreed to work together, set up a standing meeting, be it weekly or monthly. Put it on the family calendar and perhaps make it an excuse for a date night! It doesn't have to be the theme for the entire meal, but it can be a small part of the overall conversation.

## 4. Treat home finances as a business.

Home finances are the axis around which your family's security turns. Money affects all aspects of your life, and the handling of those finances is really a business unto itself. Treat it seriously. Invest in a computer program that tracks your bank accounts and begin to track your income and expenses each month.

## 5. Fess up: admit your money hurdles and where you might have miscalculated this month.

We all make money mistakes here and there. Just face them immediately. The longer you ignore the past-due notices, shortages, or overdrawn account, the worse it gets.

## 6. Don't blame each other; have a common goal to correct the situation.

As a couple you're in this together. It is "our" money. No one is to blame if you're trying to work as a team.

**Remember: fighting doesn't change your finances.**

In addition to the Money Fight, another issue factors into the family finances—the Money Shadow.

# THE MONEY SHADOW

The Money Shadow is a cold, dark secret that haunts moms at every level of income. It's the dark side of money that you're working to expose. Simply put, the Money Shadow is the financial inequality a woman experiences in a marriage. You may not be able to put your finger on it or to articulate your feelings of antsiness or powerlessness in regard to the finances of the home, but you may feel the shadow when:

You give up your paycheck to raise your children.

You share your paycheck and he's not sharing the load.

Your paycheck doesn't equal his.

You feel you need to follow a stricter budget.

You don't understand or are not privy to your long-term
investments.

You buy yourself new clothes.

You spend on something perceived as a luxury, such as a
manicure, a massage, or a facial.

You pay the household bills.

Make no mistake, the Money Shadow is real, and if left unexposed, it grows bigger and darker. That's why we are shedding light on the Shadow and hopefully making for brighter days in marriages.

## LAUREL'S MONEY SHADOW STORY

A caller into our radio show recently went back to work as a nurse. Laurel's youngest just started kindergarten. She had dedicated the better part of the past decade to staying home and raising her two children. She loved being able to stay home with her kids, but she always felt the guilt of not earning a paycheck. She says it was nothing her husband said or did; it was a self-imposed guilt.

Laurel says she definitely felt a financial inequality in her marriage. She felt the guilt of the Money Shadow when buying herself new clothes, and she felt insecure when making financial decisions for herself and the family. She says that financial inequality led to a tipping of power in the household: it was her husband who ultimately had the power to make most of the financial decisions. Again, she says her husband never said a word about it. In fact, she says, her husband couldn't be more caring and respectful. These Money Shadow feelings were coming from within.

Sunshine chased that Shadow away, however, when Laurel went

back to work and started earning a paycheck again. Even though she doesn't make as much money as her husband, she says those feelings of inequality are lessening. It's not only a good feeling for her, but she says it's been great for their marriage. Laurel says she's getting her groove back and it feels good. There's more romance in their marriage and she feels empowered.

The feelings Laurel expressed are the feelings so many of us know all too well. The Money Shadow doesn't always come from our husbands, bosses, or anyone else. Often, it's our own attitudes about money that create the Shadow. For so many years, we haven't wanted to talk about our financial feelings because we didn't want to appear ungrateful, spoiled, or resentful.

## TRACY'S MONEY SHADOW STORY

> I work as many hours as my husband, but unfortunately I make $20,000 less a year. Even though I work a full-time job, because I don't earn as much as he does, it is my duty to care for the children, buy the groceries, cook all the meals, do the laundry, and keep the house clean. My husband believes he is the main breadwinner and thus deserves to rest when he gets home, while I don't sit down until it's time to go to sleep. —Tracy

This is classic caveman behavior from John Gray's *Men Are from Mars, Women Are from Venus*. Men really think they need and deserve cave time at the end of the day, a time to decompress and regroup for the evening ahead. We love that book, but what the heck, John, they're not cavemen! Why give them excuses to act like Neanderthals? We say, keep that outdated behavior up and we're going to roll a boulder in front of the cave.

It's imperative to talk about the Money Shadow: how it makes you feel and how to shed light on the darkness of inequality. Couples need to have a Financial Honesty Hour to explore their feelings about family finances and come to a comfortable agreement without fighting.

# WAYS TO SHED LIGHT ON THE SHADOW

Laurel banished the Shadow by going back to work. But Tracy was already at work. This leads us to believe that the Money Shadow isn't attached to a paycheck or the amount of that check. It's attached to the way you think about money and how you perceive yourself. For those of you trying to get out from under the Money Shadow, the best way to start is by making the Money CASE.

**Communicate.**
**Act.**
**Stick to it.**
**Enjoy.**

**Communicate:** Talk to your husband about the Money Shadow. Explain what it is, how it has crept into your relationship, and that you would like to create a solution for it. When you take the focus off his being the problem and place it on the looming Shadow, he'll be more receptive to your concerns.

**Act:** Devise and present a plan to counterbalance the inequality around money and chores. Show him how you plan to be more involved and educated about the finances (especially retirement and insurance). It also helps to present him with a list of chores and errands that need to be done every day or every week and ask which ones he's comfortable helping with. Men, like children, want to please you, but they don't want to always be told what to do. Make them think it's their idea.

**Stick to it:** It won't be easy to change habits around the house. Don't start with the entire list of changes. Start with one. Do it for twenty-one days, then add another change, and so on.

**Enjoy:** Enjoy shedding light on the Shadow. Enjoy the fact that you and your husband are becoming more of a team working toward a common goal. Enjoy the fact that shedding light on the Shadow shows consideration for everyone in the home. Children will benefit from a house bathed in light rather than shadows.

## MomsTown Take
### on the Multiples of Money

We have multiple credit card accounts, grocery cards, ATM cards, gas cards; we also have multiple bank accounts, savings accounts, checking accounts, stock accounts, money market accounts; we have multiple mortgages and lines of credit; some of us have multiple streams of income. Cutting up some of those cards and cutting down on some of those accounts can make your life simpler—and, maybe, cheaper.

\* \* \*

For whatever reason, wives often feel less competent in money matters than husbands. In most households the Money Shadow attaches itself because women play the role of spenders. We're the ones primarily responsible for tending to the day-to-day and monthly expenses. This makes us look like the big spenders, even when we're spending on the necessities. We are the big spenders even when we're bringing in a paycheck. If you think about it, your husband's misperceptions are that he makes all this money, and all you do is spend it. That misperception needs correction wherever it's found.

Just take a look at this chart from *Money* magazine, which provides the percentage of decision-making power for men and women in diverse financial areas.

|  | Men | Women |
| --- | --- | --- |
| Investment Decisions | 73% | 22% |
| Retirement Planning | 66% | 25% |
| Buying Insurance | 60% | 34% |
| Paying Bills | 42% | 57% |
| Budgeting | 33% | 59% |
| Day-to-Day Spending | 22% | 64% |

When we look at the chart, it's interesting to see that the numbers support what we've been talking about on our radio show and with our friends. Women are forced to make the day-to-day decisions about shopping and domestic expenditures because they are dressing the children (and themselves and often their husbands), they are cooking the meals, hiring the babysitters, paying the gardeners, and making sure the dog and the cat get to the vet periodically. That's not even factoring in who handles the emergency when the toilet backs up (answer: Mom) or who gets the kids home from school when the family car breaks down.

Let's face it: most dads work outside the home and are only around during the evening hours. For this reason, few couples ever work out a realistic budget together (although the Unique You is going to lead the charge in your house), so Dad really has no idea of the debts until he looks—usually by mistake—at the checkbook or the credit card statement and goes ballistic.

## MomsTown Take
### *on the Split-Second Swipe*

A split second is the amount of time it takes to swipe your debit card at the grocery store or your credit card at the department store. These split-second swipes have a tendency to be forgotten. To illustrate this point, we coined the Five *W*s of Amnesia Spending. You forget what, when, where, why, and, most important, who swiped? (Was it me or my husband?) You forget where you've swiped. You forget how much you swiped, and you even forget why you swiped. And that leads to a rude awakening when you get the bank statements in the mail.

At the end of a day, make a list of every store, gas station, and ATM where you swiped. Did you swipe for coffee, lunch, or dinner? Did you swipe for those new shoes, or for the milk and bananas at the grocery store? When you add up your swiping, your head starts spinning, but this exercise clarifies just how much is going out of the account on a daily basis.

* * *

Now that you recognize his Man Math ways and your Lady Luck tendencies, you see those are not necessarily the best stances to take or very productive ways to solve your money problems. In fact, they help feed the Money Shadow. Here are some ways to unify your approach to money issues that we have gathered from other moms:

## Ten Money Tips from MomsTown

1. Add up the daily expenses. Carry a small notebook with you every day and record your daily spending. Do this for one week. It's the same concept when you're trying to lose weight. Health experts tell you to write down everything you eat. We're just suggesting that you write down everything you spend.

2. Spend fifteen minutes a day on personal finances. Just fifteen minutes a day with your checkbook, bank statements, and investment options can really pay off. If you own a computer, obtain a copy of the Quicken program and learn how to use it. (Don't worry about the year on the box; an older version will be just fine for learning purposes.)

3. Create a money corner. This is a place in your office, kitchen, or anywhere you can do paperwork. It should be an organized money section that has files for old bills, statements, and new bills. It should also have space for a check register, calculator, and a calendar for when bills are due.

4. Create a prosperity corner. This focuses your intention to attract more money. For example, our money corner has

candles, coins, favorite prosperity quotes on pieces of paper, and our lucky elephants with trunks up!

5. Create a vacuum. Get rid of the old. Donate it or sell it on eBay. A vacuum brings in more energy.

6. Watch what you say. Don't say, "I want more money." Instead say, "I have more money" or "I am getting more money." Want begets want and have begets have.

7. Schedule regular Money Talks with the husband. Make sure the conversation is at a good time of day and you are both in a good mood. Always keep each other in the loop.

8. Write down five- and ten-year financial goals.

9. Have an automatic withdrawal to a savings account. Even if it's a modest amount, it adds up and can turn into a family vacation or cover holiday expenses.

10. Remember money is a tool. It works for you.

# THE WITTY CHART

When Man Math and Lady Luck start talking dollars, they often end up in a fight. To forestall any misunderstandings, heated conversations, or tears, we have devised a little chart. We call it the WITTY money chart. WITTY stands for *We're In This Together, Yippee!*

This is the chart that brings Man Math and Lady Luck together. It takes the emotion out of the situation for you and allows your husband to see the situation on paper. The WITTY money chart details what's coming in and what's going out on a monthly basis. It takes the blame out of the conversation. Just the facts, ma'am.

It covers everything from the mortgage and utilities to food and pet care.

With a little luck and a little math, this spreadsheet will quickly give you more control over your finances.

| HOUSEHOLD INCOME | January | February | March | April | May |
|---|---|---|---|---|---|
| Paychecks | | | | | |
| Child Support | | | | | |
| Alimony | | | | | |
| Refunds | | | | | |
| Rental Income | | | | | |
| Other | | | | | |
| Total | | | | | |

| HOUSEHOLD EXPENSES | January | February | March | April | May |
|---|---|---|---|---|---|
| Mortgage/Rent | | | | | |
| Utilities | | | | | |
| Tuition | | | | | |
| Food | | | | | |
| Dining/Entertainment | | | | | |
| Clothing/Shoes | | | | | |
| Household Supplies | | | | | |
| Health Care Insurance | | | | | |
| Dental Insurance | | | | | |
| Eye Care | | | | | |
| House Insurance | | | | | |
| Car Insurance | | | | | |
| Life Insurance | | | | | |
| Car Payment | | | | | |
| Car Maintenance | | | | | |
| Trash | | | | | |
| Personal Care Products | | | | | |
| Travel/Vacation | | | | | |
| Gifts | | | | | |
| Holiday Expenses | | | | | |
| Gardening/Yard | | | | | |
| Pet Care | | | | | |
| Books/CD's | | | | | |
| School Supplies | | | | | |
| School Events | | | | | |
| Extracurricular Activities | | | | | |
| Furnishings/Decorating | | | | | |
| Credit Card Debt | | | | | |
| Groceries | | | | | |
| Property Taxes | | | | | |
| Income Taxes | | | | | |
| Total | | | | | |

| BUSINESS INCOME | January | February | March | April | May |
|---|---|---|---|---|---|
| Paychecks | | | | | |
| Other | | | | | |
| Total | | | | | |

| HOME BUSINESS EXPENSES | January | February | March | April | May |
|---|---|---|---|---|---|
| Computer | | | | | |
| Internet Connection | | | | | |
| Fax Machine | | | | | |
| Scanner | | | | | |
| Software | | | | | |
| Professional Services | | | | | |
| Total | | | | | |

| June | July | August | September | October | November | December | Total |
|------|------|--------|-----------|---------|----------|----------|-------|
|      |      |        |           |         |          |          |       |
|      |      |        |           |         |          |          |       |
|      |      |        |           |         |          |          |       |
|      |      |        |           |         |          |          |       |
|      |      |        |           |         |          |          |       |
|      |      |        |           |         |          |          |       |

| June | July | August | September | October | November | December | Total |
|------|------|--------|-----------|---------|----------|----------|-------|
|      |      |        |           |         |          |          |       |
|      |      |        |           |         |          |          |       |
|      |      |        |           |         |          |          |       |
|      |      |        |           |         |          |          |       |
|      |      |        |           |         |          |          |       |
|      |      |        |           |         |          |          |       |
|      |      |        |           |         |          |          |       |
|      |      |        |           |         |          |          |       |
|      |      |        |           |         |          |          |       |
|      |      |        |           |         |          |          |       |
|      |      |        |           |         |          |          |       |
|      |      |        |           |         |          |          |       |
|      |      |        |           |         |          |          |       |
|      |      |        |           |         |          |          |       |
|      |      |        |           |         |          |          |       |
|      |      |        |           |         |          |          |       |
|      |      |        |           |         |          |          |       |
|      |      |        |           |         |          |          |       |
|      |      |        |           |         |          |          |       |
|      |      |        |           |         |          |          |       |
|      |      |        |           |         |          |          |       |
|      |      |        |           |         |          |          |       |
|      |      |        |           |         |          |          |       |
|      |      |        |           |         |          |          |       |

| June | July | August | September | October | November | December | Total |
|------|------|--------|-----------|---------|----------|----------|-------|
|      |      |        |           |         |          |          |       |
|      |      |        |           |         |          |          |       |
|      |      |        |           |         |          |          |       |

| June | July | August | September | October | November | December | Total |
|------|------|--------|-----------|---------|----------|----------|-------|
|      |      |        |           |         |          |          |       |
|      |      |        |           |         |          |          |       |
|      |      |        |           |         |          |          |       |
|      |      |        |           |         |          |          |       |
|      |      |        |           |         |          |          |       |

## Resources

### DAVID BACH

*Automatic Millionaire: A Powerful One-Step Plan to Live and Finish Rich* (Broadway, 2005)

*Smart Women Finish Rich: 9 Steps to Achieving Financial Security and Funding Your Dreams* (Broadway 2002)

*Smart Couples Finish Rich: 9 Steps to Creating a Rich Future for You and Your Partner* (Broadway, 2002)

### SUZE ORMAN

*The 9 Steps to Financial Freedom: Practical and Spiritual Steps So You Can Stop Worrying* (Three Rivers Press, 2006)

*The Laws of Money: 5 Timeless Secrets to Get Out and Stay Out of Financial Trouble* (Free Press, 2004)

*The Courage to Be Rich: Creating a Life of Material and Spiritual Abundance*

*Women and Money: Owning the Power to Control Your Destiny* (Spiegel & Gray, 2007)

### DAVE RAMSEY

*The Total Money Makeover: A Proven Plan for Financial Fitness* (Nelson Books, 2007)

*The Financial Peace Planner: A Step-by-Step Guide to Restoring Your Family's Financial Health* (Penguin, 1998)

### CLARK HOWARD

*Get Clark Smart: The Ultimate Guide to Getting Rich from America's Money-Saving Expert* (Hyperion, 2002)

### APPLICATIONS

Microsoft Money

Quicken

*Chapter 7*

# Great Sex after Kids

he Sex Talk. Most couples don't want to have it. We all want our sex lives to be what they once were or even better, but we struggle with how to make that happen. We realize that if any of us are going to start having more and better sex, we better start talking about it. So, here we go.

In this chapter we're going to solve the mystery of why before kids we looked forward to sex and after kids we put it on the back burner. (Some of us took it completely off the stove. Ouch!)

> *My girlfriends tell me if I'm too tired at night and don't want morning sex, I should call my husband at work and have him come home for a nooner. There's only one problem with that: he'd show up! —Anne*

Married couples say they have sex an average of 68.5 times a year. That's slightly more than once a week.

—*Newsweek*

We moms are a tired bunch, and we find it's easier to talk about the mortgage, the kids, and the in-laws than it is to talk about our sex lives. Why is that? Sex is the reason we're all here in the first place. And in marriage, sex is a big deal. It plays an important role in our lives, and we should be talking about it openly, especially with our husbands. But most of us don't. We get embarrassed, feel shy, and are afraid to bring up what's going on behind closed doors. We understand. If you're too embarrassed to talk about it with your husband, talk about it with us. After all, what are girlfriends for?

We've been talking about sex a lot lately. We've talked with a lot of women and even with some of the nation's top sex experts. We've heard from an overwhelming number of women who are simply too tired for sex. To them, sex is just one more task on the to-do list. Their sex drives seem to be headed in reverse.

Think about that for a second; think about your sex life as if it were a car. When you were single, you were always in second gear, ready to go, your engines revving. Putting on your makeup was like filling the tank; it was foreplay, and you found the anticipation delicious. But now that you have kids, you first have to find the key. When you find the key, you have to get in and start the car. Then you need to warm up the engine, find first gear, take it around the block a couple of times, and hope that you don't run out of gas before you get to your destination.

Which brings us to our main point: how do you get to your sexual destination? To get there, start thinking like a sexual agent.

**Good sex is like good real estate—location, location, location!**

# Location #1: YOUR MIND

The first location is your head. Are you mentally in the game? The truth is you are usually just too tired and have too much on your mind. This is the dilemma facing most of the busy women we know. We are mentally and physically exhausted. It doesn't even seem to matter if you want a great sex life if your head just isn't there. And for most women, we need to be mentally into it.

We have both found that knowing our natures makes it easier to nurture our relationships. For example, the two of us are talkers, and we married talkers. We know that verbal stimulation is foreplay for us. We'd both rather go to dinner with our guys and have a glass of wine and good conversation than go to a movie. Take us to some action flick and we may be entertained, but we're more likely to just fall asleep when we get home—if not before.

Talk to us over dinner and it's a different story—with a different ending. When we go to dinner with our man, we are face to face, talking and and focusing on the two of us as a couple. At a movie, we may be sitting next to each other, but we're not at all focused on one another. A good book that helped us uncover our nature is *The Five Love Languages* by Gary Chapman. You might find some of the information relevant to your own relationship.

Women need the mental stimulation of love and romance. We miss the days of thinking about it and wanting it all the time. So, how do you get that desire back and feel like your sexy self again? First, you have to understand the reasons why you're just too tired. You have to understand the first location; you have to understand your state of mind.

> *Women love romance and feeling in love, and that is a huge precursor to sex for us.* —MomsTown consensus

When resuscitating your libido, you may find it helpful to take a mental vacation. For instance, let your mind wander off to Yellowstone

National Park. Yellowstone is one of the largest geothermal landscapes in the world. There is so much activity brewing under the surface that scientists predict one day it might erupt into a supervolcano, affecting everyone in its path. Women are true daughters of Mother Earth, and we have our own geothermal features bubbling beneath the surface. We have a lot on our minds and a lot on our plates. We're thinking about everything we did today, everything we need to do tomorrow, and everything in the near and distant future. It's no wonder that sex is not at the top of our mind. We call it the Maid, Cook, Chauffeur, and Siren Syndrome.

*When we have sex, I can't stop thinking of my to-do list. He's going to town, and I'm going to the grocery store.* —Carol

You cannot help mentally being at a different location. However, there are a few things you can do to ease the pressure and let off a little steam.

The first thing you can do is to talk about how you're feeling with your husband. A partner left in the dark is no help at all. Men need to know what's bubbling under the surface—our surface. Otherwise he might take it personally and think it's all about him, when really, it's all about you. Share the mental burden. Just be prepared for him to share his feelings as well (it could happen). We do recommend, however, to not let off this steam right before jumping into bed. It's an absolute mood killer: trust us, we've tried it.

We find it's more comfortable to have these kinds of talks during a scheduled time, a quiet time, or a time when you're both in a good state of mind. Realize that most men are not that keen to respond when we say, "We have to talk." However, if you say, "Honey, when you have a moment, I have a few questions," the results are usually much better. Initiate the conversation when both of you are calm and relaxed. Tell him you want the two of you to have a satisfying sex life (together) and ask him for his suggestions. This kind of talk might be a bit uncomfortable at first, but once you break the ice, you'll both start warming up to the idea and, hopefully, to each other.

Another way to let off a little mental steam is to write. We know you've probably heard this before, but getting it all out on paper really works. It helps you untangle the endless tasks muddling your mind. Write down everything you need to do, even long-term tasks. When you get something down in black and white, you get it out of your head.

Once you've talked about your feelings and written them down, you can engage in some practical exercises to get in the mood. The best thing you can do for your sex life is to start thinking like a woman: like a full, sexual being.

To help you free your mind, here are some ways to get into the mental game of sex:

⊙ Think erotically. When you're in a long-term relationship, sex has a way of becoming too familiar. You fall into habits—ruts, if you will. There's nothing arousing about doing the same thing in the same position every week for twenty years. Sex should be lots of things, but it should never be boring. We need to take a walk on the erotic side. Switch it up and you'll not only surprise your guy, but you'll also spark your inner Aphrodite.

---

Eroticism is the use of sexually arousing or sugges-
tive symbolism, settings, illusions, and situations in
art, literature, drama or the like. It is the condition
of being sexually aroused.

—*American Psychological Association (APA)*

---

Focus on finding ways to bring eroticism back into your lovemaking. Remember when you were dating and you looked forward to going out with him and even daydreamed about how romantic and fun the evening would be? You primped and planned for making love after going out to a concert or dinner. Well, getting into date night and really putting thought into how to make the evening even more sensual heightens your sexual tension, in a good way.

> Kevin says everyone on our block is having more sex than us. We typically do it once on the weekend. And of course, it's missionary style. My husband wants me to be more playful in bed, and I would be, but I'm too embarrassed. —Tami

## Quickie

There are hundreds of ways to be more playful and more creative about sex. Go to your local bookstore. There's an entire section on sexuality. You won't feel like you're doing something dirty, but you will get some fun and playful ideas.

- ⊙ *Get selfish.* Stop worrying if you're doing the right things; or if he is turned off by your thighs; or if you are taking too long, moving too slowly, or moving too quickly; or being too quiet or too loud. Really, to enjoy and give him enjoyment, let loose. Go to it with abandon.
- ⊙ *Aim high.* Consider doing what you did for him during the first year or so you were together. When you first begin a sexual relationship with your guy, you aim to please him. After you have kids or enough years have passed, you just hope to please, but you stop aiming so high. If you want to get his attention, aim high.
- ⊙ *Talk it out.*

*If he would just talk to me and actually listen, that would be a great turn-on.* —Janice

*We just don't talk anymore. It's like we're just going through the motions.* —Crystal

## Quickie

Often when married couples talk, it is about problems at school, problems with the checkbook, or problems with the children. You have to make a conscious effort to introduce topics that are about creating intimate connections. What did you talk about before you were married? What about vacation plans? What makes him happy? What makes you happy? Find some common emotional ground.

## Another Quickie

Next date night, make it a dinner date rather than going to the movies. Tell your husband to "make dinner your happy meal." Tell him that when he talks to you over dinner, it's a turn-on and you consider it foreplay.

---

HAPPY ORGASM DAY

A politician in a small Brazilian town declared May 9th as Happy Orgasm Day as a way to enhance sexual relations between couples.

—*Dr. Ruth Westheimer*, DrRuth.com

---

Sex is one of the most precious, intimate parts of life a couple can share. It should be treated with the respect due one of the wonders of the world. Just like at Yellowstone, there are so many pools and pockets to explore together. We find it helpful to remind ourselves that sex is not just about the physical act. For women it's about building an emotional connection. Our approach to bridging that emotional connection, however, is much different than men's. Women need intimacy to engage in sex. Men need sex to engage in intimacy. How do we know this? We hear it, we read it, and we live it. Chances are you're living it too.

The question is how do you meet in the middle and meet both your needs? Someone has to extend the olive branch, and since this book is all about you, it looks like you'll have the branch in your hand. But there will be a benefit to you. For example, we had a gal call in to our radio show. Carolyn was a little annoyed. "My husband is always nice to me after we have sex. The next day he'll call me from work, help me with the kids, and even do the dishes. Why doesn't he do that before we have sex?"

We're not sex experts, but we did have to stop and ask Carolyn, "What's the problem? Have more sex with him and maybe he'll do the dishes every day. Before you know it, you won't know what came first, the sex or the kindness."

Now, we're not saying to use sex as a bartering tool, but if you like the results and it's improving other areas of your relationship, why question it? Just go with it, leave him love notes all over the place, give him a little phone sex during the day, and you might even get the garage cleaned out on Saturday. Problem solved.

Yes, it's true what other experts tell you—that if you just start having sex, you'll get in the mood. We accept that and know that to be true, but our goal is to be in the mood before having sex. Not only is it more fun and more satisfying, it builds more intimacy between us and our guys. As well as we can tell, our men (at least, most of them) don't want us to just *start*. Men get a lot of satisfaction out of knowing that we're anticipating a good time and that they are pleasing us. In the mental game of sex, you can get the sex life you're craving when you're open-minded.

Here's how we and other MomsTown moms are making up our minds to get in the mood.

# SEX CHEAT SHEET: GETTING YOUR HEAD IN THE GAME

## Quickie #1:
### THINK ABOUT SEX

Thinking about sex is easy. Men, it seems, are unable to *not* think about sex. To focus your mind on it, pick up a magazine like *Cosmopolitan*. *Cosmo* is always a good choice for this topic, since sex seems to be all over the cover. The *Cosmo* of today is not the *Cosmo* we read as teens. Isn't it funny when you're at the salon and you pick up a woman's magazine and you quickly realize it's not just the blow dryer heating you up?

## Quickie #2:
### FANTASIZE ABOUT SEX

Pick up a romance novel. All you have to do is read about some cowboy riding up in a tight pair of Wrangler jeans to save the day. We believe romance novels are written for the explicit purpose of getting women in the mood. In fact, if husbands understood more, they'd buy us a subscription to *Cosmo* and a lifetime's worth of Harlequin romance novels.

Can you even imagine what the world would be like if both men and women had the same sex drive and preoccupation with it? Nothing would ever, ever, ever get done. It actually strikes us as a bit unfair. Why can't women have the problem—or pleasure—of thinking about sex all day long? Why do we have to be the ones who go through all the work to bear the children and then suffer from lagging libidos. What's up with that?

## Quickie #3:
### FANTASIZE ABOUT SOMEONE ELSE

Hey, even Jimmy Carter lusted in his heart. Fantasy is a great way to get yourself started, even before your husband arrives on the scene. The object of your fantasy doesn't have to be a movie star—or anyone real, for that matter. That's why they call it fantasy. Note of caution: Fantasizing too much about the pool boy or someone else's husband is generally not a good thing. Immediately buy yourself some steamy romance novels and get into some studly heroes who are not three-dimensional.

## Location #2: YOUR BODY

Sex happens in your body as well as your mind. Start with a quick list of questions about your own body.

1. Do you know what you physically like?
2. Do you know what turns you on? And does he know?
3. Are there other physical barriers preventing you from having good sex? For example, are you feeling self-conscious about your body? Are your hormones playing with your emotions and your physical self? Describe how you feel about being a physical sexual being.

In our conversations with women, we know that when we start describing how we feel physically, we come up with ideas about how to enjoy sex more often. We hear that there are many factors—physical, hormonal, mental, and relational—that can impact our sex drives and ultimate enjoyment. Let's start with what seems to be most on our minds, the physical aspects.

Is your lack of sex drive really a physical issue? Partly. Your body is not the same as it used to be. And most likely you don't feel as comfortable in your skin as you used to. Your belly is not as firm, your breasts are a different consistency and shape. You're exhausted, and you're possibly stretched out, so your orgasms perhaps don't feel as intense as they did before. Other issues that doctors tell us could be affecting women are scar tissue, which can cause us pain, a weakened pelvic floor, prolapsed organs, and incontinence. Not an attractive reality, is it?

But you can work with this. You can get rid of the mirror in your mind's eye that assesses you so cruelly on a daily basis and replace it with a kinder, more accepting mirror that appreciates the vehicle you were given to grant life. Pretty heavy, huh? Well, no pun intended but a good message.

**Let's stop judging ourselves and start embracing our curves.**

If you don't like your belly, then perhaps you should stop before you bite into food you know will go straight to your midsection. Also, instead of being annoyed with your thighs and derriere and wishing you could Photoshop them right out of your jeans, start moving 'em every day with some exercise. Even if your shape doesn't change considerably, you'll feel stronger and healthier, and here's the bonus: exercising and sex are very similar, and they both make you feel sexier.

Is your problem hormonal? Could be. A hormonal contraceptive can affect your free-flowing testosterone. (Okay, that sounds like we know what we're talking about, but speak to your health practitioner about this.) Also, pregnancy and breast feeding have an effect on your libido. In

**Information You Need to Know . . . or Maybe Not**

We were amazed to learn from Dr. Laura Berman, PhD, relationships expert and director of the Berman Center in Chicago, that you can exercise your vagina to move it up, down, forward, backward, and even side to side. We exclaimed, "What? Side to side?" Yes, side to side. Imagine the possibilities in bed!

fact, Dr. Laura Berman says for your sex drive to get back to normal after nursing, you need to give your body six months to regulate. After discontinuing hormonal contraception, your body needs three months for your hormones to bounce back. And even women in their early forties can begin to experience menopausal symptoms that change their sex drives.

## Quickie

Tell your doctor that your sex drive isn't what it used to be. Modern medicine and alternative methods can be successful at putting a zip back into your hormones.

> I have worked with thousands of women over the past several years. Homeopathy has helped even the most challenging cases of PMS, menopause, and other hormonal issues. Even women that are on hormone replacement (HRT) feel added support from homeopathy and are able to take this healthy route to feeling balanced and whole again. You do not need to suffer from symptoms or side effects anymore. —Homeopathic expert Allison Maslan, HHP, CCH

> Several months after the onset of menopause I experienced exhaustion and depression. I wasn't able to attribute it to anything personal, nor could I attribute it to my thyroid since I had just been tested. I was very weepy and very sad, and no matter how much mental effort I put into giving myself positive affirmations, I just couldn't pull out of it. Then four days after trying homeopathy, I pulled out of the depression and felt my energy increasing. I have been doing great for several months. I didn't realize how badly I felt until after I had taken the first dose. It was like night and day . . . my old self was back again! —Carole

Sex and all the intimacies that go along with it can either save a marriage or ruin it.

> Sixty percent of husbands and forty percent of
> wives will have an affair at some time in their
> marriage. That explains why more than fifty
> percent of marriages end in divorce.
>
> —*Peggy Vaughan*, The Monogamy Myth

Are we really a culture of sexually obsessed individuals who can't control our urges? Or are we just not getting what we need out of our current relationship? Sex experts say both men and women will be tempted to stray when their sexual and emotional needs are not being met. As we see it, men typically need sex and women need emotional connection.

## SOME AMAZING SEX STATISTICS

Statistics show that many women would rather go shopping than have sex. In fact, lots of women around the world, as it turns out, would rather go out with their friends than have sex (Durex Survey, 2001). Also according to the Durex Survey the average married couple has sex 98 times per year.

Perhaps this is why: according to Robert W. Birch, PhD, in *Pathways to Pleasure*, only 35 percent of the female population will orgasm during intercourse. Does that mean 65 percent of us aren't having an orgasm during intercourse? No wonder we're not interested in seducing our husbands.

And here's another statistic that will startle your man but certainly not you: 48 percent of women admit to faking an orgasm. Frankly, we're surprised the number is so low.

\* \* \*

Try to talk about sex in a positive way as often as possible. It's easy to gripe about it with your friends, joke about how tired you are, how men are just sex-crazed and think about it all day long. But the truth is, if you keep joking about it in a negative way with your gal pals, you'll be joking your way all the way to divorce court. If that happens, you'll find another man, and unless you change the way you think and talk about sex, you'll end up in the same position as you started.

You've heard the adage, *Wherever you go, there you are.* You might as well work on what you have, right here, where you are.

## SEX CHEAT SHEET: GETTING YOUR BODY IN THE GAME

### Quickie:
#### GET OVER YOUR BODY

Yes, you. You with the ponytail and sweats on. Figure out how to make tonight the night, and lead the charge. Feeling too fat to tango? Don't be so hard on yourself. Even if you're feeling fat, flabby, and self-conscious, he's not holding those extra pounds against you. He just wants you to relax and feel good with him. Let yourself go and enjoy what you're doing.

> *I have anxiety about my breasts. I used to have great breasts, but now they don't stay up when I take my bra off. And they don't feel the same anymore. They're soft and mushy; how sexy is that?* —Carin

> *Why is it every time I get in bed with my husband, he rubs his hand across my belly? I know where that hand is headed. I wish he'd just skip my abs altogether. It just reminds me of how many sit-ups I need to be doing, and it ruins the mood.* —Leigh

So your body isn't what it used to be. Women seem to have many more physical hang-ups than men. You need to get over your physical insecurities and self-criticism and start enjoying yourself as a sexual and sensual woman. You were built for sex too. This is where those talks come in handy. Believe us, by the time he gets to the belly-rubbing stage, he *really* doesn't want to ruin the mood, so he's not doing it to make you feel bad. But he won't know it's a turn-off for you unless you tell him.

## Quickie:
### FLIRT

Rub his back, touch his arm, compliment him, and hug him. Start out slow. It can start with a wink of an eye. It may feel uncomfortable at first; it's possible you may startle him! But heck, the payoff is worth it. There is a whole slew of books on sensual touch. Check out the *Kama Sutra*. Flirting is another form of foreplay, so start winking.

> *I don't even know if he sees me anymore. He hasn't paid me a compliment in years.* —Holli

## Quickie:
### GET SOME DISTANCE

Ask yourself, "When was the last time I complimented him?" After many years in a relationship, you can fall into a place of familiarity and forget to "see" your partner. Stand back and observe him at a party or an event. It's an effective way to create distance and see him as the man you fell in love with.

# Location #3: YOUR ENVIRONMENT

Okay, Lady, the third location we want to visit is your environment. This is probably going to be the easiest location to navigate in our sexual tour. We've explored ways to improve the mental and physical aspects of our sex lives, and now we're going to start exploring new territory (literally). It's possible that the only sexual hang-up you are having is your bed. Get out of it, and have sex somewhere else. Try having sex at a different time of day, in a different setting, with different scenery.

Having sex is just like riding a bike. You have muscle memory. Having sex in the same location and in the same position is like pedaling round and round the same block. There's no thrill. The thrill is gone because your body has already anticipated what's about to happen. Get on a mountain bike and head out on a mountain trail, and you'll automatically feel more of a rush. You're still riding a bike, but the experience is completely different! It'll give an edge to an otherwise boring ride.

Here's how some of the women we know are spicing up their sex lives with a little location manipulation.

> We actually had sex in the car the other night on the way home from a movie. We felt like we were in high school again. It was a little more awkward, but heck, we figure with a little more practice, we'll be going to the movies a lot more often. Talk about a happy ending! —Stacy

> I'll never look at our patio furniture the same again. —Mariana

> A late-night romp on the sofa is always comfortable yet, for us, feels a little risky. It's definitely not an every-night escapade, and that's kind of exciting. —Ellen

Now is a good time to take a look at your environment. Think about where and when you could surprise and seduce him. If you're not ready to venture outdoors or to another location, there are things you can do to spice up your bedroom.

# BEDROOM QUICKIES

## Throw your television out the bedroom window.

According to Italian sexologist (now that's a fun job!) Serenella Salomoni, "We need to get the television out of the bedroom. When we do this, our frequency of sex is going to double." We agree! Late-night television is not a turn-on. Sorry David, Jay, and Conan. However, the right late-night programming may just be what the sex agent ordered.

## Romance the room.

Going back to the River Runs Through It theory, remember that each room in your house evokes a feeling as you enter it. What is your bedroom saying? Is it cluttered? Does it have mismatched bedding? Are clothes strewn everywhere? One lamp burnt out? Lots of books on the night stand? If so, that will give the bedroom an unsettling chaotic feeling. It will also serve as a distraction to your love life. The bedroom is for sleep, connecting with each other, and sex. If you romance up your bedroom to say "Let's do it," you'll heat up your sex life.

## Remove the mirrors.

Yes, we know that some people consider them real turn-ons. Okay for them. In general, however, mirrors are distracting and make us self-conscious. Get rid of them—unless you want to hang your mirror horizontally for your full viewing pleasure.

## Think in twos.

For the other parts of the room, think two candles, a picture of two people, ideally you and your mate, and not your kids or—God forbid—your inlaws. That's just not right!

## Think in hues.

Bedroom colors should evoke warmth and cuddly feelings. Using blues in your bedroom will cool things down. Use warm, subtle tones such as beiges and golds.

## Shut the doors to any adjacent rooms.

One of the quickest things to take the wind out of your sexual sails is the sight of a sleepy child who has just awakened at night. It's okay, Mom and Dad, to put a lock on the door, and if you must, put a monitor in the kids' rooms. Your bedroom is a sanctuary—for the two of you. Closed doors. Privacy. Intimacy. Get it?

## Candlelight, candlelight, candlelight.

Enough said. Vanilla is a great scent for romancing the room.

## Get the bed right.

Don't place the bed under a window. Make sure your bed has a direct view of the door. Don't store boxes or other stuff under the bed; it's like sleeping on baggage. The less baggage you take into the bedroom, the better sex life you'll have. Have a solid headboard for your bed. (Gotta have something to grab on to.) If you divorce, buy a new mattress and headboard.

# THE MARRIED HOOKUP:
# RECONNECTING AS A COUPLE

Let's face it: life after children is different. From a philosophical point of view, you take your place in the great linked chain of mankind. Through your children, you come to a new appreciation of your parents and the decisions they made. You see yourself as not just another pair of kids "hooking up" for the night, but as people who have made a joint commitment to roles in your family, both immediate and extended. You have a richer understanding of individual growth and, perhaps, of the concept of history itself.

Sex probably will never again be as thrilling or as passionate as those wild, spontaneous encounters of your younger self. However, some married couples learn that sex is worth exploring on a different level than what they experienced when they were single. Those people agree that they want sex to be an important part of their married lives, and they are willing to plan, experiment, and explore the infinite possibilities of different kinds of physical pleasure together.

Many of the MomsTown suggestions can be an excellent start to making that reconnection as a couple. However, the challenge—and the fun—is that you as a couple must find your own way, at your own pace, with your own unique desires. Making "the beast with two backs" is surely a universal human experience, but each couple finds their own special way.

We're not suggesting that you immediately begin trying every position in the *Kama Sutra* (although that's an intriguing thought). On the other hand, one of the best ways to reignite the engines of love is to learn more about it and just think about it. For guidance on your journey, check out the Resource section books (our favorites are Anne Hooper and Alex Comfort) and websites.

If you both commit to trying to reconnect sexually (and we've never heard of a husband who wasn't willing), you may discover that it is easier than you feared to merge the two worlds of husbands and wives. We all go into marriage with the hope that this is it. Our husband is the one for us for eternity. Then, after the children are born, we all wonder how we got to this point. Where did our inner sex kitten go? Is she gone forever, replaced by a mom in mom jeans? Or can we revive the little kitty? The good news is that we talk to all sorts of women who are bringing passion back to their relationships. You can do it too.

## Resources

*Rekindling Romance for Dummies* by Ruth K. Westheimer (For Dummies Books paperback). What can we say, except that this diminutive lady is the most outspoken expert on sex. She spells out lots of good ideas in her books. You don't even have to be a dummy to get rekindled by it. Her website is www.drruth.com.

*Sex: The Manual* by Anne Hooper (Ellipsis Arts paperback). This is a thorough, thoughtful, and sensible presentation of sex by a longtime expert. Hooper has written many books on the subject (including the most intelligent and sensitive reading of the *Kama Sutra*), and her knowledge is well represented here. She has a website: www.annehooper.com.

*The Joy of Sex: 30th Anniversary Edition* by Alex Comfort (Pocket Books paperback). This is the book many friends have given each other for wedding presents over the decades. You don't have to believe everything Dr. Comfort says, but he certainly makes many varieties of sex sound joyful. Copiously illustrated.

*The Secrets of Sensual Lovemaking: The Ultimate in Female Ecstasy* by Tommy Leonardi (Signet paperback). Ummmm. This is sort of a graduate course in sex. It may be more than most couples are ready to brave. On the other hand, if you want to explore new frontiers . . .

*The Five Love Languages: How to Express Heartfelt Commitment to Your Mate* by Gary Chapman (Northfield paperback). Working on the theory that many of us use different language to express ourselves, Chapman, a professional marriage counselor, offers lots of options and encouragement for each to find his and her own words. It works for us! His website: www.fivelove languages.com.

Allison Maslan, HHP, RSHom(NA), CCH. Her website is www. homeopathicwellness.com.

*Passion Prescription: 10 Weeks to Your Best Sex Ever* by Dr. Laura Berman, PhD, Director, Berman Center, www.Bermancenter.com.

# WE ALL MARRIED THE SAME MAN

We know that when we're able to talk freely with friends, without fear of judgment, we are able to find peace, solutions, and even humor in our shared experiences. After all, it wasn't until we started opening up with each other and other friends that we realized that when it comes to sex, we all married the same man.

How do we know? Consider this:

- We want more sleep. He wants more sex.
- We want to talk more. He wants more sex.
- We want to be cuddled and hugged. He wants more sex.
- We want him to connect. He wants more sex.
- We want to talk about our feelings. He wants more sex.
- We want to go out to dinner. He wants more sex.

# Chapter 8

# Girlfriends, Hookers, and Chicks

---

One loyal friend is worth ten thousand relatives.

—*Euripides*

---

Okay, we're going to admit it—we haven't always been friends. The first time we met, we knew we had a lot in common. We knew we shared the same vision for our business, and in fact, we went into business together within a week of our first meeting. But were we friends? We'd have to say no. What's funny, though, is we sure sounded like it. Our business venture had us sharing a radio microphone, and we sounded like we had known each other for years, but we were faking it. We weren't even really sure how much we liked each other. We knew, however, we were a good team.

Jump ahead a few years, and we realized that our friendship was becoming more important than the business. Wouldn't you figure, just like a couple of women: our friendship is more important than the bottom dollar? You bet. That's one way you know you are really friends.

There are all kinds of reasons why women become friends, and each friendship is unique. But one thing that is common among women is that we all have a vital need for girlfriends. Girlfriends keep us young, keep us laughing; they shed tears with us, and they help us solve problems. Girlfriends help us in every aspect of our lives.

---

The loneliest woman in the world is a woman without a close woman friend.

—*George Santayana*

---

Friendship is a topic that is right at the heart of MomsTown. When we ask the women on our message boards, "To whom do you tell your innermost secrets?" the answer is rarely "My husband." Don't get us wrong. There are lots of confidences and private issues that a husband and wife keep between them and the pillows on their marital bed. Ideally, your husband should be one of your best friends. But there are some matters that women only feel comfortable discussing with other women, and they need to discuss them.

Medical studies conclude that friends can help keep us healthy. According to a study at Harvard Medical School of more than 100,000 female nurses, women with friends stay healthier as they get older. The researchers even go on to say that not having friends is as detrimental as smoking or obesity when it comes to our overall health.

You need to connect with girlfriends in order to work through your fears, worries, and concerns, and to stay young. Nothing makes you older quicker than stress, and friends are amazing stress relievers. Women are constantly seeking ways to connect with one another. Women need other women. In fact, at a recent upscale gala, a table full of fortysomethings were joking that life would just be easier if they would all become lesbians. That's not a joke aimed at men or gay women; it is a humorous expression of a deep truth.

---

Sometimes I wonder if men and women really suit each other. Perhaps they should live next door and just visit now and then.

—*Katharine Hepburn*

---

Let's get right to the point: here are some of the many ways that the MomsTown moms describe friendship:

- You have someone who listens.
- You feel like you're close by, even if you live hundreds of miles apart and haven't spoken in weeks.
- You can remember those little things you did years ago.
- She's honest with you but not judgmental.
- You can count on her to help you out in a bind, like watching your kids or lending some sugar.
- She does nice things without ever thinking about getting something in return.
- You have someone to go out to lunch with or do other things with like go to the movies or a concert or eat chocolate and drink wine.
- The benefit to having a friend is to be able to do things for someone else and feel as though you are appreciated for helping.

It's the friends you can call up at 4 a.m. who matter!

—*Marlene Dietrich*

# BUILDING FRIENDSHIPS

One of the many truths about getting married, having kids, and going through the many changes in life is that your friendships change. Think about it: think about how many friends you have lost contact with and how many new friends have entered your life.

Losing a friend is never easy. Even if the end of the friendship has been gradual, we feel a loss. It can hurt, but sometimes it's necessary. We'll discuss more about ending friendships in a moment, but first, let's take a look at positive ways to build friendships.

There may be a friendship you didn't expect in your near future. We have discovered from our own personal experience and from the advice of other women the top twelve ways to keep friends and make new ones:

# TWELVE TIPS FOR MAKING FRIENDS AND KEEPING THEM

1. Be a friend. To have a friend, be a friend.
2. Be a good listener. Listening may be the most important part of your friendships. There is often more joy in listening than in hearing yourself talk. It lets you know you're needed. You should love to hear about your friends' lives. You should like to be a part of their life story.
3. Be a talker. Communicate. Let your friends know how you feel. Communication should relax you. Talk is emotional food

for your female soul. It sustains you. It makes you feel good. When you aren't able to talk, you starve. It's not because you need to vent or gripe—although it's great to do that. Talk equals connection. It gives you hope and makes you feel wanted.

4. Loose lips sink friendships. When secrets are shared, keep them.

5. Be supportive. Be encouraging. Wherever two or more women are gathered in the name of friendship, therein is a support group. It's one big happy therapy session. It's even better than going to a therapist, because a true friend will dish and drink with you. Also, moms share so many of the same issues, they can come up with answers to the problems that plague you.

   "I am lucky to be here tonight," Jen told her two best friends from high school. "I thought about bailing on you two, because I feel like I've been beaten over a rock. I'm exhausted, but I knew I would feel even worse if I didn't make it. Do you guys ever feel like you just want to go to bed at eight o'clock every night?" Jen's friend Mindi replied, "Absolutely. You just need to make up your mind tonight that things will start to be different tomorrow. Why don't you start by going to yoga with me Thursday night? You've been talking about it for the past year." Jen thought about her friend's response. Thursday night she went to yoga, and she tells us she's been going just about every week for the past fifteen months. She loves it, she has more energy, and she tells us she loves her friends for noticing that an eight o'clock bedtime was not the answer.

6. Share ideas. Share your enthusiasm. Positive exchanges build positive foundations and it's a great way to start a friendship. Women are full of brilliant and creative ideas, and you can get energized by bouncing your ideas off them. Ideas for making

money, decorating, and losing weight without exercising or giving up any food make for great girlfriend brainstorming sessions.

*One of our favorite pastimes is to brainstorm new business ideas. We haven't actually gone into business yet. We both already have full-time jobs outside the home, but one of these days one of our ideas is going to click. —Mari*

7. Remember, you're not perfect and neither are your friends.
8. Do nice things without expecting anything in return.
9. Be yourself. Be authentic. Don't try to be someone you're not just to be friends. A friendship built on false identities will fail.
10. Stay in touch. We're big advocates of sending e-mail. It's quick, it's easy, and it lets your friends know you're thinking of them. A handwritten note, a phone call, a lunch date, or getting together for whatever reason is always a good idea.
11. Open your heart. It may feel risky and it is. There's always a chance of rejection. However, when you open your heart and it is received, a true friendship emerges.
12. Laugh together. Norman Cousins and UCLA research teams proved that laughter has many medical benefits, including lowering blood pressure, strengthening the immune system, and relieving stress.

---

Friendship is born at that moment when one person says to another: "What! You, too? I thought I was the only one."

—C. S. Lewis

---

## A MomsTown Take
### on The End

There will be friendships that end. Some will come to a screeching halt and others will fade out over time. There are several reasons why friends go their separate ways. However it happens it's usually always painful for everyone involved. Here are some stories of friendships that have ended. Names have been changed to protect the innocent and not-so-innocent.

## WHEN THE KIDS AREN'T A GOOD MATCH

I met Jani at our kids' elementary school. Our kids hit it off immediately. One day, however, I caught her daughter pushing my daughter around. That night my daughter said she's afraid of her friend because she's always yelling at her and telling her what to do. Apparently, this behavior had been going on for some time. I told her that she didn't have to be her friend anymore and that a real friend doesn't make you feel bad. The next day, I told Jani our kids didn't have good chemistry together and that my daughter is afraid of her daughter. She was surprised to hear it and didn't understand why I took it so seriously. She said, "Kids will be kids." I know that's true, but I believe it's important that we teach our children how to choose friends. I couldn't tell my daughter to ignore the behavior and try to be friends. It was hard for me. I lost a friend. I really enjoyed Jani, but in the end, the lesson I taught my daughter is more important than my lost friendship. —Lesley

# WHEN YOUR FRIEND IS TOO GOOD OF A MATCH

I caught my best friend in bed with my husband. Both of those relationships came to an end. I let my ex-husband keep the bed. —Sara

# WHEN YOU GO FROM BEING SINGLE TO BEING A COUPLE

Lilly and I have been friends since college. I got married and had a baby, and our lives were different. I was no longer interested in the single scene, and when I didn't want to go out with her on Saturday nights anymore, she told me I had turned into a boring housewife. Maybe I am, but I'd rather be holding my baby on a Saturday night than holding her hair back. —Danielle

# WHEN YOU MOVE

Carly and I live in different states now. I'm really kind of surprised that we don't stay in touch anymore. I guess we're both just really busy. She has a lot of other friends, and I'm starting to make new friends. I hope she's doing well. It would be nice to talk to her again, but I don't know what we'd talk about. Is that strange? —Veronica

# WHEN SPOUSES DON'T GET ALONG

I used to have the best time when I was with Olivia. We could talk and laugh for hours. Then we had the brilliant idea of going on a double date with our husbands. What a disaster! Our men were not into being there at all. They were polite to one another *but the tension was there. Unfortunately, it kind of put a damper on our friendship. Truth is, I didn't really like her husband and she didn't like mine. That date was the beginning of the slow death of our friendship.* —Holly

The best way to cope with the end of a friendship is to focus on the elements of a friendship that bring out the best in you. And it's important to realize that there can be varying degrees of friendship. But always remember that women need girlfriends for many reasons; however, the primary reason is that we have an insatiable need to have emotional connections to others. To fulfill that emotional need, you need someone to talk to and someone to listen to, someone to give advice to and someone to get it from, and someone to brainstorm and to gossip with.

Yes, we said gossip! We know gossip is not supposed to be a good thing, but why is it we all do it? We can't help ourselves. Does that make us bad people? Absolutely not! Because gossip can have its good side too.

We've come to realize there are two kinds of gossip: guilty gossip and virgin gossip.

## GUILTY GOSSIP

This is the kind of talk that makes you want to take a shower. You know it's malicious, and it just makes you feel bad. It makes you feel bad saying it and hearing it. And if the subject of your gossip heard what was being said, you would feel ashamed for even being present during the gossip session. Basically, guilty gossip is talking smack about someone else. For instance, you repeat a rumor that is destructive to the subject, such as, "Your married boss is having an affair." Even if it's true, what's the point of repeating it?

Be aware that when you're guilty-gossiping, the person you're gossiping with feels just as guilty, even if she's reveling in the dirty laundry. We've all taken part in guilty gossip. The key is to red-flag it and halt your words before they are uttered. Guilty gossip should be stopped in its verbal tracks.

## VIRGIN GOSSIP

On the flip side, virgin gossip is the kind of gossip that is pure and innocent. It's the problem-solving gossip. It's benevolent talk, benign comments or observations that are about someone else. The key is that it doesn't make you, the speaker, the listener, or, most importantly, the subject feel bad. For instance, you say, "Oh, I heard a rumor that Cindy and Bob just bought a new house." Even if it's true, it doesn't make anyone feel bad, especially Cindy and Bob. Virgin gossip can also be a great tool for problem solving. For example, we were just talking the other day about how a girlfriend of ours lost fifteen pounds last year and has been able to keep it off. We were talking about how great she looked and wishing we could drop some pounds.

She wasn't present, but we used her as our subject, and we'd been gossiping about her waistline for the previous two days, trying to figure out how she did it. We admit it, we were talking about her. We each had bits of information from her that we had been able to pull together. Wouldn't you know it, her plan involves drinking more water, cutting the sugar and bread from her diet, and exercising. Our virgin gossip led us to the conclusion that we need to stop eating M&M's and get to the gym more. Problem solved.

## WHY HOOKERS ARE SO SMART

Whenever we think about the importance of girlfriends, we think about the smartest hookers we know. The Happy Hookers is a group of older women that Heather's grandmother belongs to. They have been meeting every Thursday since the 1960s. This is a special community that knows how to fight growing old. They call themselves the Happy Hookers because they meet every week with crochet hooks in hand, and the happiest day of their week is Thursday. Heather (and every one of her cousins and her cousins' kids) has crocheted blankets and afghans to prove it. If you don't have a crocheted blanket of your own, no worries; we have some hooker wisdom that is sure to keep you warm.

## FIVE HOOKER LESSONS

1. Girlfriends save marriages. We're not talking about his girlfriend. We're talking about yours. True friends help you through the tough times of marriage, simply by listening (and not always offering advice) and being there when you're not feeling that marital bliss you think you should *always* feel.

2. Girlfriends mend broken hearts. When devastating events happen, girlfriends are there. Girlfriends are there after the divorce and after the funeral; they are there when family members let us down.

3. Girlfriends share secrets. You can tell a true friend what you're ashamed of, embarrassed by, or scared of. You can also tell them your innermost hopes and dreams.

4. Girlfriends share stress. They'll drop everything, they'll be there for you, and they'll help you find solutions. Girlfriends also pray for each other and let each other know they're not alone.

5. Girlfriends share laughter and gossip. Whether they're laughing at themselves or laughing with you, the key is they're laughing. And when it comes to gossip, you better be there on girls' night or you might be the topic of that week's virgin gossip.

# THE ETHEL PRINCIPLE

Several years ago, we used the friendship between Lucy and Ethel on *I Love Lucy* to illustrate the value of girlfriends; we called it the Ethel Principle. Some people have told us we should update our Ethel Principle. But how do you find better girlfriends than Lucy and Ethel? No matter what kind of crazy circumstance they found themselves in, they always had each other as backup.

We were accused of being old-fashioned. We were told that we needed a little *updating*. So, we put out a MomsTown request for a replacement couple. We asked women to give us suggestions of a pair of girlfriends who could replace Lucy and Ethel.

Here are the suggestions we got, along with our thoughts:

**Laverne and Shirley**
> Does that make it the Shirley or the Laverne Principle? All we hear in our heads is "Don't call me Shirley."

**Thelma and Louise**
> Would be a great one, except the ending has us a bit worried. Seems a little dramatic.

**Monica and Rachel**
> Their friendship got canceled before they became moms. They're out.

**Cagney and Lacey**
> A bit intense, a little rough around the edges, and who wants a girlfriend who has to carry a gun?

**Kate and Allie**
> This pair is the best contender so far.

When it comes down to it, Lucy and Ethel had six seasons and have never been off TV and they are still in syndication. Plus, we have all the T-shirts already made up. We'll stick with Lucy and Ethel. Discussion over. Thanks for playing.

## A MomsTown Take
## *on Girlfriends*

You have someone to go to when no one else is there! Sometimes you go through things in your life that you just don't want to tell your hubby or other family members. With girlfriends (true girlfriends) you know you can bare your soul and they will go to the grave with your secrets. Girlfriends can help you by sharing that they go through similar situations. They are there when you need a laugh or need to cry. Girlfriends help you grow, and true girlfriends will tell you where the bear poops. Best of all, you know they are only trying to help you, not tear you down. —Laura

# THE CHICK FACTOR

The word chick, when not being used to describe a baby chicken, has come to mean in contemporary slang a particular sort of young woman. The masculine usage implies cool, attractive, and, adding further confusion, chic. Sometimes, it is used by men as a broad generic for women.

For most women, on the other hand, chick has a negative connotation. It suggests those days of high school, when in the interests of propping up your own ego, you constantly compared yourself to others and tried to be "hotter than thou."

We doubt that you need a definition of the Chick Factor, but here it is anyway! The Chick Factor is the sizing up of women that other women do. But here's the thing about the Chick Factor: there's a little Chick Factor in all of us. Let's face it, it might be uncomfortable to do so, but we can't help checking each other out. Women look at each other's figures, clothes, shoes, and men. We're instantly judging and drawing conclusions. We compare our lives, and sometimes we just can't help it. We know it should be left to the high schoolers, but even us thirty- and forty-somethings do it. The key is to recognize it and try to stop it as often as possible. Or at least try to put the chick in a good light.

There is a famous quote by Eleanor Roosevelt that we try (as hard as it is) to keep in mind when the Chick Factor starts chirping in our heads: "Nobody can make you feel inferior without your permission."

You shouldn't feel bad about yourself just because someone else has more money, a better figure, a bigger house, or a fancier car. For example, we have a friend who is always running and fasting and basically has a nightmare of a figure and she's almost fifty! We're not kidding; she looks great in a pair of size 26 designer jeans. She buys size 26 because she "likes her jeans *loose.*" What the heck! If we wore a size 26, they'd be glued to our ba-hookie. Anyway, we confess: we apply a lot of the Chick Factor on her by looking for some flaw, basically because she deserves it for telling us a size 26 is too big for her. The Chick Factor says, "Don't get too big for those 26 britches, we're about to level you." Now is a good time to remember Eleanor's quote. When we see "26," Eleanor's insight is our mantra.

Eleanor would tell us we're giving her size 26 jeans permission to make us feel bad—and that's our fault.

## FOUR TIPS FOR RECOGNIZING THE CHICK FACTOR

1. You meet a new woman for the first time, and she instantly looks you up and down, and she doesn't even do it discreetly. Blatant chick! She's looking at your shoes, your clothes, *and* your roots.

2. When she smiles, you don't see her teeth.

3. She gives you a limp handshake and says, "Mmm, hmm, nice to meet you."

4. She brags about her size 26 jeans and how she needs to work more on her abs.

## A MomsTown Take
### *on Best Girlfriends*

*My best girlfriend story is simple. I have one friend that I have been close to for over fifteen years. We have been through a lot with each other; marriage breakups, births of babies, being homeless, deaths in our families, being together on our birthdays because they are close, and just about any life crisis or celebration you can think of.* —Helen

# THE "WE MUST BE FRIENDS" TRAP

Another pitfall in women's friendships is the "We must be friends" trap. This is the expectation many women have that we must be friends with everyone we know. We regularly anticipate that we will like each other. We are surprised when we don't. For some crazy reason we take it as a personal offense if we meet someone who doesn't want to be friends. The "We must be friends" trap is a problem many women create for themselves. For example:

- We both have two-year-olds, *we must be friends.*
- Our kids go to the same school, *we must be friends.*
- We work together, *we must be friends.*
- Our husbands work together, *we must be friends.*
- We're neighbors, *we must be friends.*

Of course, when new friendships arise under any circumstances, they should be welcomed and treasured. But don't fall into the foolish trap of thinking that proximity is friendship. All women need to hold high standards of loyalty, compassion, and genuine connection when choosing friends.

# WHERE DO YOU FIND FRIENDS?

Having just pointed out the dangers of assuming friendships on the basis of similar situations, we have to admit that sometimes those situations are the meeting places of lifetime friends. The truth is that you can make friends almost anywhere—from the local coffee shop to your office. You just have to be open to friendship. That nineteenth-century New England sage Ralph Waldo Emerson said it well: "The only way to have a friend is to be one."

Many women, particularly women with small children, feel isolated from regular society and ensnared in baby talk all day long. We've had many messages in MomsTown to that effect. Happily, some of those moms, who have never met, find solace in virtual friendships.

A quick word of advice: whatever you do, *never* Google "need girlfriend." Holy buckets! We did it when we were looking for women blogging about their girlfriends, and wow, it's amazing how many *ladies* want to be our girlfriend—in an, *ahem*, physical way.

Women need connection and it doesn't have to be face to face. We see this connection taking place online every day.

> *My best friend and I have never met face to face. We started working together online about five years ago and have never stopped talking to each other since day one. I know if I need a listening ear, I can call her, e-mail her, or IM her and she will be there for me and vice versa.*
>
> *I know I can call Karly day or night with a problem or to vent and she does the same. Sometimes we correspond for hours about nothing and sometimes about everything. The one thing I wish is that Karly and I could meet one day face to face. She lives in Arkansas and I live in Ohio. We write about it all the time. —Sandra*

Friendship, and the potential for friendship, is all around you. Sometimes it pops up in very unexpected places. Who would have thought that a virtual friendship would have lasted so long? It's our hope that one day Karly and Sandra will meet in person, but until then we wish them a happy virtual girlfriendship.

---

Friendship with oneself is all important, because without it, one cannot be friends with anybody else in the world.

—*Eleanor Roosevelt*

---

Not all friendships are as healthy and encouraging as you would hope them to be. We're about 100 percent sure that you have friends in your life who have a tendency to distract you from your potential. You might have a friend that constantly depletes your energy and takes from you without ever giving back. Remember, friendship is a two-way bridge. That bridge connects your two lives, and you should generally try to meet in the middle. Of course, it doesn't always work out that way; sometimes one friend has to travel farther to the meeting place, and that's okay. However, if you're the one always giving and your friend is always taking, it may be time to call the whole thing off.

## YOU CAN BE FRIENDLY WITHOUT FORGING A FRIENDSHIP

The reality of friends is that they change, they grow, and sometimes they grow apart. Keep in mind that it is possible to be friendly without having to be close friends with everyone.

Do I want to be friendly with everyone I know? Yes.

Do I want to be friends with everyone I know? No.

It may seem strange, but remembering these two questions helps you shed guilt and be yourself. Trying to be friends with everyone you know is exhausting and phony. Friendship implies closeness, trust, confidentiality, and intimacy. You simply can't have that with everyone you come across. That doesn't mean you can't get caught up in a conversation, have coffee, or take phone calls from acquaintances; it just means that you shouldn't put pressure on yourself with the belief that you have to like everyone and that everyone has to like you. When you accept this fact, you can be more yourself. You don't have to put on airs to impress or try to maintain an emotional connection. It's okay to just smile, wave, and keep on walking.

---

No person is your friend who demands your silence, or denies your right to grow.

—Alice Walker

---

## FRIENDSHIP RED FLAGS

There are reliable signs when a relationship is failing to fulfill a positive role in your life. You do not need to look for trouble, but you need to be aware that problems can arise. You then have to make a decision either to distance yourself from a negative relationship or to work with the person who is failing you. In our experience, the latter rarely works because those people are acting negatively because of personal issues.

**The Downer.** This is the "friend" who brings you down every time you talk to her. She makes you feel bad for feeling good. She's weak and whiny. She's a victim in her own life and can't make anything change. She wants you to share her pain and live it with her. She is too caught up in her problems to even notice that you might have a few of your own. In this relationship there is no reciprocity.

**The Exhaler.** She never stops talking long enough to let you speak, let alone take a breath. This friend is the center of her own universe and you got sucked into her vortex. Blow her off.

**The Edgy Girl.** This is the "friend" who always makes you feel on edge. She's too private; she's too judgmental; she's sarcastic in a mean way; and you can never let your guard down around her. When and if you do, you'll pay for it later.

**The One-Way Woman.** Simply put, this gal is high maintenance. She always expects you to call her. She forgets that her phone dials out. And not only does she expect you to always call her, drive to her, meet her one-way, but she also gets upset when you don't. She expects you'll do things for her and she doesn't reciprocate.

There are no scorecards in friendship, but don't be afraid to let go of girlfriends who only deplete your energy and never fill you back up again. You should look forward to your time with friends as time you are free to be yourself.

# THE MEANING OF TRUE FRIENDSHIP

There are plenty of ways that friends can fail you. Conversely, there are many more important ways that friendship among moms can nurture and energize your life.

> A true friend is the most precious of all possessions and the one we take the least thought about acquiring.
>
> —La Rochefoucauld

We want to conclude this step on the journey to the Unique You by emphasizing the positives, the joys, and the constructive help that a true friendship can offer. Naturally, for help, we turned to the girl-friends at MomsTown. Here are some of the aspects of true friendship that they treasure:

## True friends . . .

- will tell you when you're wrong. And you're a true friend when you don't hold it against them.
- will call you on the carpet when you're pretending to be someone you're not.
- believe in your dreams and want them to come true. And you believe in their dreams and pray for their dreams to come true.
- tell you when you're being too hard on yourself.
- tell you when it's time to leave him and understand when you don't.
- help you through a crisis, make you laugh, and realize this too shall pass.
- bring you dinner when you have babies, surgeries, or hard times.
- drink wine and eat chocolate with you.
- understand your annoyance when your husband flops on the couch every night after work because he "just needs a little downtime."
- totally get why all you want to do at night is sleep.
- tell you when you need to update your wardrobe.
- let you relax and completely be yourself.
- help you clean up after a dinner party.
- don't need a phone call from you every day, but can't wait to talk to you.

Time passes, life happens, children grow, and so do our friendships. We make more room for the women in our lives when we realize they are the pillars that keep us standing when things go bad, keep us laughing when nothing is funny, and keep us dreaming while we're awake. So, what are you waiting for? Give your Ethel a call.

National Women's Friendship Day is the third Sunday of September.

## Resources

50 Best Girlfriend Getaways in North America by Marybeth Bond (National Geographic, 2007)

Girlfriend Getaways, You Go Girl! And I'll Go Too, 2nd edition, by Pam Grout (Globe Pequot, 2005)

*Chapter 9*

# Feel and Look Younger Now

*W*henever we start talking about age and beauty, we realize how easy it is to start tearing ourselves apart. We can find every infinitesimal flaw on our bodies. We can hone in on every wrinkle, dimple, and sag. It's so easy to do, and before we know it, an otherwise new and sunny day has turned into old and tired beauty flogging. Let's face it, for whatever reason, it's easy to beat ourselves up over our looks.

> There are days I look at pictures from five or ten years ago, and think: "Damn, you were hot." Seriously, I just look much healthier and AWAKE. Was this before kids? Yes. But I can't blame them for everything. —Heike

Apparently we're not the only ones having a tough time reconciling ourselves to the fact that we're getting older. The moms on our

MomsTown forum and the gals who call in to our radio show all say the same thing. We wish we could just find the one miracle cream or pill that would make us look fresh-faced and put a bounce in our step.

When we get into our beauty flogging mode, we start complaining that our jeans are too tight, our hair is going gray, and what in the world were we thinking substituting baby oil for sunscreen when we were teenagers? That's when we swear we're going to drink more water, exercise, get more sleep, eat more vegetables, stop the caffeine, lay off the chocolate, oh, and take our daily vitamins. Seriously, we really promise these things to ourselves. We must admit we're good for about a day or two. Then we go back to our old bad habits and repeat the cycle.

Stand up straight. Our friend Jason Walton, an exercise physiologist and trainer, says, "It'll look like you took three inches off your waistline if you would just stand up straight."

So, what are we busy moms to do? We're all in the same boat: we're all getting older. We can't escape that fact. What we can escape, however, is how we think, what we say, what we do, and how we carry ourselves. We do have the power to look and feel younger. We are going to take a look at how you can change things on the inside and make practical changes in your daily routine to start looking and feeling younger today.

## STARTING ON THE INSIDE

Let's start with finding the power in the way you think.

When you become a mom, a million changes seem to take place in your body. We've certainly addressed all the changes you go through regarding your identity, work, sex life, and relationships, but now it's time to take a look at the changes in the way you look. We know that giving birth does a number on the waistline, changes breasts forever, and can even change the texture and color of your hair, not to mention shoe size. Your whole life has changed from the inside out. It's no wonder that when you look in the mirror, you see some things that are familiar and other things that are just out of whack. Our goal is to help you be kinder and gentler with yourself and your new look. You can make changes—we have some great practical tips for that—but the first goal is to start seeing yourself in a new way. We want you to see the beauty in the body that birthed your baby, just as you see the beauty in your babies.

Your mind is a powerful tool in helping you to look and feel younger. The female body is a work of art, so start treating yourself as such. Keeping this in mind, let's start thinking like one of the most celebrated artists of all time. Let's think like Botticelli.

## THE BOTTICELLI VIBE

Feeling comfortable with your curves is what we call the Botticelli Vibe. The Botticelli Vibe says love your body, own your creative power, and express your femininity.

Sandro Botticelli was a famous Italian Renaissance painter who celebrated mother and child. Many Renaissance painters are known for celebrating full-figured feminine beauty. We decided to take this as a huge compliment to motherhood and the motherly body.

Just as Botticelli acknowledged the feminine body, we encourage you to do the same. Keeping in mind that the best way to look and feel young is to exercise, eat well, drink lots of water, and wear sunscreen, we also want to glorify our feminine curves. If you think your butt is too big, it's possible, but it's also possible you're being too hard on yourself. Women are spending thousands of dollars to get that rebound figure. The key is to think good healthy thoughts about your body.

## GET THE B-VIBE

Let's start with what you think about. Thinking beautiful thoughts has a direct impact on how you look. So, think about everything that is beautiful about you. Think about how kind and/or generous you are with people. Think about your volunteer efforts. Think about the compliments you pay to others. Think about your life's possibilities. Think about all the wonderful things you do for your family. All of these positive thoughts add up in the beauty formula.

## FOUR WAYS TO THINK BEAUTIFUL

1. **Embody your body.** Stop hating your body parts. Thighs, bellies, arms—they're all a part of you, and when you hate even one part of yourself, that's not healthy. So, next time you catch yourself saying, "I wish I could get rid of my thighs," stop and embody those thighs. Find one thing positive about that body part even if it's just the fact that those thighs help you get up the stairs.

### Quickie

Stand naked in front of the mirror and say positive things about your body. It may be uncomfortable, maybe even embarrassing at first, but the more you do it, the easier it becomes.

2. **Visualize the body you want.** There is truth in the saying *You become what you think about.* The quickest way to improve your body image is to start thinking positively about your body.

## Quickie

Every day visualize how you want your body to look. Even if it takes cutting out a picture from a health magazine to use as your muse. Visualization is another powerful mental tool. Professional athletes, artists, and performers use visualization to achieve their desired results. You can do the same.

3. **Think mojo.** Be bold and feel like a woman—confident, powerful, and female. Enjoy your feminity, even if that means putting a little wiggle in your walk.

## Quickie

Wearing new and sexy undergarments can make you feel beautiful. It's your sexy secret that puts a sashay in your step.

4. **Attitude enhances your lookitude.** Having a positive attitude will have a positive effect on the way you look.

## Quickie

Smiling (even for no reason) takes years off your face. And smiling is one of the best and fastest ways to improve your mood.

# DON'T LET EMOTIONS UNDERMINE YOUR BEAUTY

There are a lot of emotions that chip away at how pretty you feel inside and how good you feel about yourself. Some of those emotions are fear, impatience, guilt, worry, anger, insecurity, depression, powerlessness, self-doubt, and negativity. Wow! Sounds like a lot. We're not trying to drop an emotional bomb on you, but it's important to stop and consider how these negative emotions are making you look and feel. To help you get past some of these emotions, follow this four-step process.

## Step #1: IDENTIFY THE CAUSE

Take the time to figure out what situation or life circumstance is bringing out a particular emotion. For example, if you hate your job, you may experience anger, powerlessness, negativity, and depression. You need to figure out if it's your career, your boss, a coworker, or your salary.

## Step #2: CONFRONT YOUR EMOTIONS

You've decided that you do love your job but feel you should be getting paid more.

## Step #3: DEAL WITH IT

Come up with a plan on how to ask for a raise. Determine your worth and schedule an appointment with the boss.

## Step #4: CHANGE IT

You cannot deal with an emotion if you aren't willing to make a change. The mere act of asking for that raise is a confidence booster and a huge stress reliever.

\* \* \*

It's okay to feel these emotions. It's only natural to feel them. If, however, any or all of these emotions are overwhelming you and you feel as though you have no control over them, then it may be a good idea to schedule an appointment with a therapist or your health practitioner.

# LISTENING TO WHAT YOU'RE SAYING

The other part of the beauty formula is how you talk. We call it beauty language. It's how you talk about others and how you talk about yourself. For example, guilty gossip is not beautiful, and when we take part in it, we feel uncomfortable and mean, and that makes us feel unattractive. We all know what it feels like because we've all gossiped. It's a beautiful thing, however, to recognize guilty gossip and stop yourself.

Self-deprecation run amok gets old really quick. It's nice to be humble but not at the continual expense of your self-esteem or your beauty. Words have power and force behind them. When you talk about hating parts of your body, you're talking about hating parts of yourself. Your body and soul are not mutually exclusive. One is the vehicle and the other the precious cargo.

# BEAUTY LANGUAGE SUBSTITUTION CHART

| When you hear yourself saying . . . | Say instead . . . |
| --- | --- |
| I look old today. | I look good today. |
| I look fat. | I'm looking thinner. |
| I am exhausted. | I have energy. |
| I'm overwhelmed. | I've got it under control. |
| Life is hard. | I believe in possibility. |

# ACT TO BE BEAUTIFUL

The final part of the beauty formula is to take action. If you really want to start looking younger and feeling younger, then today is the day to make some changes.

It's one thing to say you wish you looked younger or that you should lose twenty pounds. It's another thing to do something about it. It's not easy, and there are days when you'll fall short of your promise to yourself, but achieving youthfulness and good health takes tenacity and consistency. The reward is that your new, younger-feeling habits become a part of your daily routine.

## Beauty Quickies

**Hair time-out.** Overprocessed and overwashed hair is like overworked moms. We all need a little time-out from the daily grind. A great start is to not pressure yourself about washing your hair every day. Give your tresses a much-needed respite from blow dryers, flat irons, hot rollers, and everyday washing. Give your hair a break and add in a good hair conditioning treatment once a week.

**Neck, hands, elbows, knees and toes, knees and toes.** (Feel free to hum along.) Nothing will give away your age faster than a wrinkling neck, dry hands, rough elbows, and neglected feet. To keep the illusion of youth, treat your hands, knees, elbows, and toes the way you treat your face and neck. Cleanse, exfoliate, and lather on the moisturizer.

**So sweet, so soft.** Sugar mixed with oil is a great home recipe for exfoliation. It's also a great way to avoid spending a fortune at the cosmetic counter.

\* \* \*

Exercise, eating well, and getting enough rest are beautiful acts. You have the choice to feel beautiful. You can decide right now to embrace a youthful lifestyle, because make no mistake, we are talking about lifestyle. It is a lifestyle choice to not exercise and to stock the pantry with processed-sugar-packed, trans-fat-laden, no-good-for-you, disguised-as-nutritious food products. Likewise it is a lifestyle choice to work out on a regular basis, eat healthy foods, and set a great example for your children. Honestly, if you don't want to look and feel younger for yourself, do it for your kids and your family. They deserve to have you healthy and feeling your best.

> Show your loved ones you care about them
> by taking care of yourself. Otherwise, they will
> be taking care of you when you get older.
> —*Dr. Michael Roizen*

On our radio show we get the chance to talk with some of the top doctors in the nation. One of them is Dr. Michael Roizen, best-selling author of *You: The Owner's Manual* and *Real Age: Are You as Young as You Can Be?*

During our interview he gave us tips on how to stay looking and feeling younger even when we're chasing around young ones or trying to wrap our brains around the fact that our young ones are driving or getting ready to head off to college. One issue that affects women daily is a lack of energy. To increase our energy Dr. Roizen recommends implementing these fundamental health tips:

- Schedule sleep. You should be getting a minimum of six to seven hours of sleep a night.
- Walk thirty minutes a day, no excuses.
- Eat for a younger body. Try incorporating foods that will help your brain stay young, like nuts, fish, soybeans, olive oil, nut oils, fish oil, flaxseed, avocados, tomato juice and spaghetti sauce, and real chocolate (at least 70 percent cocoa).
- Floss every day. Flossing breaks up more than 500 kinds of bacteria. It decreases the inflammation in your arteries. Dr. Roizen says it will actually keep your heart pumping and your sex life thriving. (We're flossing and so are our husbands.)
- Use sunscreen. He recommends SPF 45.
- Dr. Roizen also recommends that women over forty take an aspirin a day (162 milligrams) to look and feel younger. He says it's been proven to prevent cardiovascular disease.

⊙ And finally, the fountain of youth is apparently flowing with, you guessed it, water. Staying well hydrated will help keep your body and mind youthful. He says water helps things slide though our system; it fights bad breath; it's good for our skin and our mood.

The doctor adds that this is a lifestyle change, so you should start slowly, and eventually your energy, health, appearance, and overall outlook on life will improve.

## MUFFIN TOP

Have you ever had a pair of jeans that made you feel like a rock star? Then one day you put them on, and you could barely still button them. What the heck? You yell, "What was that rolling over the top of my jeans?" Lady, that was your muffin top.

Once you've identified it, you'll never eat another one. Trust us, that moment wrecks muffins altogether. We can't even look at a muffin or a scone without thinking #$%@ muffin top! And Oprah thought mom jeans were a problem.

## CONSISTENCY IS KEY

Here's the truth: the one thing that holds most moms back from exercising and eating right on a regular basis is the busyness of our lives. And what a catch-22 it is: most of us need the energy from exercise and a healthy diet to keep pace with our demanding schedules. You may be saying, "Yeah, tell me something I don't already know," and you may be tired of having let yourself down in the past. Why do we know this? We've been there and we sometimes still visit.

## Consistency Quickies

⊙ Put your workout on the calendar. You're more likely to work out if you write it down and schedule it as an appointment. For the times when something comes up and you can't make all of your appointments for the week, establish a stick-to-the-minimum policy. The minimum should be a thirty-minute brisk walk every day.

⊙ Write down your goal. Is it to fit into a certain pair of jeans? Is it to lose ten pounds by the end of the year? Goals should be realistic. Start with small goals for immediate success. Once you enjoy the taste of success, you'll want more.

⊙ Get the family involved. Ask your husband and kids to join you on a walk after dinner. Share with them the healthy changes you want to make as a family. Tell them why you want more vegetables and fruits in the daily meals and how drinking water is good for them. Get them involved in cooking healthy meals. Kids love to taste foods they prepared. Have each family member establish their own exercise and nutrition goals, and then support one another in achieving those goals. Take pride in health.

⊙ Realize the true reward will not be a bowl of ice cream or a new pair of jeans, the reward is how great you'll be feeling.

I started eating really healthy about a week ago. My diet before wasn't that bad. But in the past week I cut from my diet caffeine, sugar, and carbohydrates. I know it sounds boring, and I have to say I had a pounding headache for about three days. So much so, one afternoon I could barely see, it hurt that bad. On the fourth day, after my body got over the caffeine and sugar withdrawal, I realized I had lost only one pound, but I felt as if I had lost ten. I felt amazing! —Kendra

# MOMS PUTTING THE MEDIA ON NOTICE

We're moms and we're not going to take it anymore!

We are tired of media messages that damage our self-image and the self-esteem of our children, particularly our daughters. We recently wrote a column about pop tarts that we want to share with you.

Unfortunately, we're living in the age of pop tart culture. Here, in an excerpt from one of our newsletters, is our take on the tart culture.

## TIRED OF POP TARTS

Out of respect for our daughters, future daughters-in-law, and women in general, we feel compelled to take a stand against pop tarts. "What's a pop tart?" you might be wondering. They are the girls (we hesitate to call them women owing to their lack of maturity) we see in the media every day. They are the girls our girls are exposed to online, on television, in magazines, and on the radio. They are the young women who, even born with a silver spoon, choose to behave badly on a regular basis for the return of fame and more money. They are dripping in couture, accessory dogs, and "look at me" attitudes. What message are they sending to our young girls and boys? Do we want our girls to aspire to these shallow depths and our boys to date and (God forbid) marry a pop tart?

We believe, and please correct us if we're wrong, that it's better to be known by ten people as a woman of quality and substance than to be known by millions as a pop tart. Now you might be thinking this is the ranting of a couple of feminist women, prudish moms, and what-have-you. Whatever we might be labeled, we believe it's time someone takes a stand on the side of integrity and on the side of women and girls who don't want to be force-fed unhealthy pastries.

**True beauty is smart, confident, poised, and articulate.** True beauty is as unique as each individual. It is our belief that there is a beautiful woman growing inside each girl. It is our responsibility to protect girls and teach them the difference between smart and tart. It's okay to teach them to voice their opinion, take a stand, and have their own style. Following the latest craze and posting unkind words or inappropriate pictures on MySpace.com is not the way to achieve long-lasting beauty or to get the kind of attention they might really be wanting.

Now that we've stated the problem, how do we, as a society, fix it? We hear from moms and dads about the pressures being put on our youngsters. It's the kind of peer pressure we never experienced. First, teach your children that they are better than that behavior, not that they're better than someone else. As Grandpa used to say, "You ain't better than nobody, and ain't nobody better than you."

As a parent, watch the trends. You don't want your kids to get caught up in the bling of tart culture. Be aware, be educated, and know what is going on in your kids' worlds.

This is in no way an attempt to stifle creativity or take away the right to free expression. However, a Chihuahua is a pet, not a brooch, and deserves to be treated as a loved member of the family, not an accessory. We're not going PETA on you, but come on, let's get real, and let's celebrate smart girls with style, not stupid girls with an "I'm better than you" attitude.

Here's a sampling of the responses we received after we posted this column in our newsletter:

> I just had to write and thank you gals for the "pop tarts" message in this newsletter! As a Girl Scout leader of girls in grades 4–6, and a mom of 11- and 5-year-old daughters, I'm seeing more and more of how this influences our girls, and not in a good way. I appreciate the stand you are taking—our girls need strong role models, and not these little bits of fluff. I'm very grateful. Thanks again, for putting this out there! —Jonetta

> Wow, thanks for the great essay on helping our girls (and boys) be critical of what they see in the media. This will be the topic of my classroom (grades 7 & 8) tomorrow, for sure. I'm interested in knowing their ideas of how to reject the shallowness of fame and

*fortune that they are bombarded with daily.* —Kathleen, mom and teacher

## COSMETIC SURGERY: AN INSIDE LOOK

Now that we've put the media on notice and have decided that we're not going to try to live up to unrealistic and plastic standards, we do want to point out that cosmetic surgery can do a lot of good. Amazing new techniques can help you look a lot younger. Cosmetic surgery is no longer just for the super rich and famous; it's becoming more affordable.

Dr. Scott Miller, FACS, a renowned plastic surgeon in La Jolla, California, who has joined us on our show to answer questions from his number one demographic, moms, knows the issues. Women in their late twenties to midforties with young kids are turning to cosmetic surgery now instead of waiting until their three-year-old turns eighteen and heads off to college. Apparently, moms are unwilling to take the wear and tear lying down. Dr. Miller says women tell him they feel a disconnect between what they see when they look in the mirror and how they feel on the inside, and with that disconnect they don't feel like themselves. If you fall into this category and are considering cosmetic surgery, Dr. Miller says you need to know these three things:

1. Friends and doctors are your best sources for plastic surgeon referrals.
2. Interview three doctors. Fewer is not enough, more is just confusing.
3. Be problem-oriented and seek an opinion. For example, tell the doctor what your problem is and let him or her tell you the solution. Dr. Miller says a lot of patients come in with their minds made up about which procedure they need. Let the doctor guide you, and then trust your gut.

# THE LOOK OF A CHAMELEON

For moms, this is an exciting time when it comes to age and beauty. We have an opportunity to pull off a lot of different looks. Throughout your life, you might be career woman; a mom playing on the playground; a parent going to a school event; a woman enjoying a date night with her husband; or a mom shopping for groceries.

**When you're a mom, you don't have to have just one look.**

It is entirely appropriate to look like a mom when you drop your kids off at school, and it's also entirely appropriate to put on makeup and look drop-dead sexy when you go out on date night. The trick is not to look like you're going out for a romantic evening when you're volunteering at the school. That is not cool. And it's not a good look. We are role models for our children and we're role models for each other. Femininity, elegance, and motherhood will never go out of style. Therefore, we are chameleons who change our looks many times a day, as our roles change.

# PASS ON THE STYLE
# TO OTHER GENERATIONS

Beauty and your outlook on looking and feeling younger are gifts you can pass on to your children. Your beauty has an opportunity to live on for generations to come. If you think beautiful thoughts, say beautiful words, and do beautiful acts, you will pass on your feelings about beauty to your children and your children's children. What a gift!

## Resources

### BOOKS

You, The Owner's Manual: An Insiders Guide to the Body That Will Make You Healthier and Younger by Michael F. Roizen, MD, and Mehmet C. Oz, MD (Harper Collins, 2005)

You, On a Diet: The Owner's Manual for Waist Management by Michael F. Roizen, MD, and Mehmet C. Oz, MD (Free Press, 2006)

### WEBSITES

More tips and advice from Dr. Roizen: www.realage.com

Dr. Scott Miller, www.millercosmeticsurgery.com

American Society of Plastic Surgeons, www.plasticsurgery.org

American Board of Plastic Surgery, www.abplsurg.org

American Academy of Dermatologists, www.aad.org

Jason Waiton, exercise physiologist and personal trainer, www.jasonwaiton.com

# Chapter 10

# Hold Your Family Close

If you ever start feeling like you have the goofiest, craziest, most dysfunctional family in the world, all you have to do is go to a state fair. Because five minutes at the fair, you'll be going, "You know, we're alright. We are dang near royalty."

—*Jeff Foxworthy*

*E*very family has its own issues, its own characters, and its own ups and downs. No one can know more about your family than you. What we can discuss and what we do discuss with women every day are the common threads that run through every family and how to deal with them.

First, a lot of families (and ours included) seem to be getting caught up in this Twenty-first-Century Frenzy. We are living in some hectic times. The pace is fast and furious for us and our kids. We all seem to be running at Mach speed in different directions. We are all on each other's speed dials, and we're in such a rush, we're lucky to sit down together at the dinner table.

**For most of us, this is *not* how we were raised, and it's causing us a lot of discomfort.**

We were raised in a slower-paced world. When we were kids, there were no remote controls, answering machines, or cellular phones, and

### Statistics on the American Family

Only 25 percent of American households consist of what most people think of as a traditional family: a married couple and their children (www.unmarried.org).

The United States is the world leader in fatherless families: fully 30 percent of all American families have only one parent; 8 out of 10 times, it is a single mom (www.rainbows.org).

More than half of all American marriages end in divorce (Women's Educational Media).

Which means that 50 percent of all children will live with a single parent (usually Mom) at some point in childhood (2000 U.S. Census).

Of all children in chemical dependency hospitals, 75 percent are from single-parent homes (www.rainbows.org).

Of teenagers who become pregnant, 75 percent are children from single-parent homes (www.rainbows.org).

Nontraditional families are the norm. More than half of Americans today have been or will be in a stepfamily situation (Women's Educational Media).

There are 2.4 million grandparents acting as the primary caregivers for the children in their families (Women's Educational Media).

There are between 6 and 10 million children of gay, lesbian, and bisexual couples in America today (Women's Educational Media).

we're sure this whole road rage deal is a fairly new phenomenon. The trouble is we're all moving fast, we're constantly being bombarded from every direction, and our homes and our lives are overflowing with too much stuff. There seems to be a lot of pressure to keep up with the new pace and to keep up with the Joneses.

Sure, the Joneses have always been in the neighborhood, but they didn't have so much stuff. Today, it seems as though so many have so much. Our kids have too many toys, our mailbox has too many bills, our inboxes have too many messages, and we're just surrounded by too many people in too much of a rush. How does family time fit into our busy schedules? Over the years, we've gathered some of the best advice from the experiences of other moms and the knowledge of experts to help us build strong families, raise good kids, and be good moms.

In addition to the stuff, we have too much on our calendars, too much on our minds, and our families are paying the price. We talk with women who are afraid we are losing close family ties—the kinds of ties that came from sharing joyous moments together. Today, when there's an available moment, instead of coming together, family members are slipping into their own private universe. The private universe is that personal world created by each and every one of us. It's that world where we're talking on our cell phone in the car even though our kids are in the backseat. But they don't seem to notice because they're either listening to their iPod or entranced with their Game Boy.

## A MomsTown Take on Cell Phones

I had taken the boys to get a sandwich at the local deli. I was sitting there with my seven- and six-year-old when two teenagers (a brother and a sister) came in the door. They both walked in talking on their cell phones. They didn't bother to get off the phone even when they placed their orders. They placed their orders to go.

*With sandwich bags, drinks, and cells in hand, they headed out the door. The brother went first. He opened the door, let himself out, and the door swung back and hit his sister, causing her drink to spill down the front of her. She gave him a "you jerk" look. He didn't even bother to apologize. The amazing part of this whole transaction was that neither of them even bothered to get off their phones.* —Matti

They were each in his or her own world and didn't seem to notice or care about the person two feet away from them. Private universe is a problem. The solution starts with the family universe.

## MomsTown Quickies
### FOR BUILDING THE FAMILY UNIVERSE

These tips come from our community of online moms:

1. *Spend less time on the Internet.* —Kami

   It may seem ironic since this tip came from our website, but we agree: when your family is around, spend less time on the computer. If our kids see us connected online, they see us disconnected from them. Then they want to be on the computer, they disconnect, and it just becomes this sad cycle of separation.

2. *Limit the amount of time kids are allowed to play video games and watch television.* —Beth

   We know families that have gotten rid of the television altogether. Some haven't watched TV in eighteen months. They say that at first it was hard, but now no one misses it, not even the teenagers.

3. *Spend quiet time in the evening together as a family.* —Darla

Use the time to do homework and to read. We all gather in the family room. Sometimes the kids are finishing up their homework while Mom reads a magazine and Dad works on his jigsaw puzzle. It's really peaceful, and you may notice that your kids will do better in school.

4. *Give your kids a time limit for talking on the phone.* —Marcia

We know moms who set daily limits. Twenty minutes a day or 400–500 minutes a month seems to be about right.

5. *Take family walks together after dinner.* —Alicia

A little fresh air, a little exercise, and another fifteen minutes together. It is worth doing, even if it's just around the block.

6. *Family-only day trips are a great idea.* —Sally

So often we invite other families and friends to help us entertain the kids. However, when we go with just our immediate family, we have more intimacy and family sharing. The kids play better together and we have a chance to talk.

7. *Go on family vacations as much as possible.*

*Every time we go on vacation and leave the kids behind, my husband and I say to each other, "We should have brought the kids." And every time we go on vacation and take the kids, we say, "What were we thinking?"* —Molly

Although we may joke about not wanting to take the kids, most of us are doing it anyway. According to travel experts,

when Mom and Dad head off on holiday, they're taking kids too, and they're willing to pull them out of school to do it. According to the *Wall Street Journal* (November 9, 2006),
61 percent of travelers say they would take their children out of school for a family trip, up from 45 percent in the year 2000. This trend reflects a shift in values toward more family time.

8. *Involve everyone—kids included—to create a family history.* —Elaine

You don't need to be a genealogy expert to begin with how Mom and Dad met and the events that happened when the kids were babies. Many schools encourage children to interview Grandma or Grandpa about their lives. You might be amazed by the family bonds that are built when you and your children explore your common heritage.

## CORE STRENGTH

When we're at the gym, we're always being told to work on our core strength. Apparently, core strength is important because it gives us the stability a bottle of chardonnay can't. All kidding aside, when we're strong to the core, we're able to function better in all aspects of our life. The same could be said for our family. The strength of our family relies on the core of that family. Nowadays, that core could be a mom and a dad, a single mom, a single dad, or anyone primarily responsible for loving, supporting, and nurturing the family. Nowadays, there is no one description of family. But we know, no matter how your family shapes up, that there needs to be core strength, and that strength begins with you, the mom. When the stability of a family begins to falter, the children are the first to know—and the first to suffer. They may feel the emotional impact but have no understanding of the adult issues. Parents don't have a choice; we must find ways to resolve our differences or problems and to give our children the unconditional love and support that they deserve.

Faced with the bleak reality that half of all American marriages end in divorce, if you and your husband want to stay together, then you have to work to stay together. The stress and strains of contemporary life can quickly take the romance out of any relationship. You have to work together to keep romance alive and to nourish a continuously growing relationship, or unfortunately, one of you will no longer want to be together, which is the beginning of the end of your marriage. (By the way, according to almost every woman we've ever talked to, the D word emerges—either in thought or in argument—in every marriage. That alone does not signal the end, but it is a major danger sign that both of you better get to work on the relationship.)

## MomsTown Marriage-boosting Quickies

- This is going to sound really dumb, but after agreeing with your husband that the two of you need to work on your relationship, you should try not to use the word "work" again. Make it fun. Make it adventurous. Make sure that you are rekindling all the good elements that attracted you to each other in the first place.
- Let's face it: one of the first things that brought you together was sex. We've got a whole chapter on how to liven up your sex life, so we won't repeat it here. However, make room for the power and importance of sex in a marriage—and make it enjoyable for both of you.
- Skip trying to counsel each other. That only leads to fights. Instead, try to do some things together that you both enjoy. Horse races? Hockey games? Bridge tournaments? Hiking? Set aside the time.
- Talk together about your dreams, your goals. Have you always wanted that getaway cottage in the mountains? Dying for the two of you to go to Paris? Make plans together.

Take steps toward a family future or islands of adult enjoyment.

⊚ We're big fans of date night. Once a week, we get dolled up (and, with any luck, rested up) for a romantic evening with our spouses, whether alone or bowling with friends or holding hands at a movie. Mom and Dad see each other too often at the end of frazzling days. We've got news: neither of you is at his or her best at those times. Without mentioning the word, on date night you should *work* just as hard as you did when you were single to "get" this guy—even though you've already got him. Men love to have their egos stroked just as much as we do.

⊚ Share the joy of your children with your husband. You may have to cajole him or help him at first, but there's nothing like a sleepy child in pajamas listening to Dad read (for the hundredth time) that favorite book to make a guy burst with fatherly pride. Later on, there's soccer and Little League and plenty of other dad duties that he might have to be gently prodded into. Some men don't need any prodding, but if your guy does, a little gentle push will have him thanking you in the end.

## MomsTown Tips
### ON RELATIONSHIPS WITH YOUR KIDS

The following tips may sound a lot like common sense, and they are. However, they're also good reminders. With your days so busy, it's helpful to be reminded to slow down and appreciate your children and your relationships with them.

⊚ Tell your children you love them every day.
⊚ Hug them every day.
⊚ Look them in the eye and listen to them.

- Ask them questions and value their answers. For example, ask them a question about how to fix a problem and let them solve it—perhaps with a little help.
- Respect their feelings. They don't always feel the same way we do on a given day. There will be days when they're sad or happy and you may be feeling the opposite. Let them have their feelings.
- Let them know home is a safe haven. Kids should feel secure at home. They shouldn't have to come home every day to another round between Mom and Dad.
- Do projects together. Let them help with dinner (especially cleaning up).
- Give kids responsibilities. Kids love to know they're helping and needed.

# TRUTHS ABOUT FAMILY

It must also be added that each family is unique. And each family has to find its own way to work together. Today, a frequent phenomenon is the extended family, the group of people around you and your children that may be closer to you than blood relatives.

**You inherit your family, but you choose your friends.**

There are single-parent families, "blended" stepfamilies, foster families, unmarried families, gay and lesbian families, and others we've probably missed. Every family has different kinds of support groups and close friends because of the diversity of the many kinds of families today.

There can be no doubt of the uniqueness of each family unit, but there are deep and valuable truths that we all share and need to remember. Your family is in this together. Through the excitement, challenges, drama, and routine, you want more peace. You want to achieve peace every day no matter what is going on. Peace is not perfection. Peace is the overall feeling that everything is going to be okay, that even if you're going through a hard time now, it will get better: when your child turns twenty-five, he will be kind and be able to read and write. And we all want to know how to enjoy our family life. We all want to find more peace at home.

You ask yourself, how do I enjoy each day a little more? How do I relax about the future? And how do I ever know I'm making the right decisions along the way? Finding those answers begins with recognizing ten fundamental truths.

## Truth #1: YOUR WORLD REVOLVES AROUND YOUR FAMILY

Your family life is the axis of your existence. It's the reason you work, worry, and plan for the future. So, when you're feeling stressed, overwhelmed, and chaotic, your world tilts. You get knocked off balance and you can't give your best. You forget things when you go to the grocery store, you can't concentrate at work, and you begin to feel vulnerable, guilty, tired, and anxious. When something has to give, it cannot be the family. You must accept this truth. It will make your job of prioritizing a lot easier. You can work less, spend less, do less, clean less, and enjoy more. And never forget how important you are to your family universe.

## Truth #2: MOMS CAST AN AURA

Women have a silent power. You may think you have superpowers (you wish you had Samantha's bewitching powers: boy, would your house be clean!), but you don't. However, you do have an aura. That distinctive quality and character shapes the atmosphere of your home. You are missed when you're not home, and your presence is the invisible glue that binds the family together. Recognize this power and recognize the impact you make every day. When you're stressed and chaotic, your family is stressed and chaotic. If you stay calm and focused, chances are that your family will do the same.

## A MomsTown Quickie
### ON KIDS AND STRESS

> *Kids don't have perspective on the stress in our lives. Thank God they are too young and innocent. But I know that my kids feel it when I feel it. So I try to take a moment in the car or wherever to calm myself and prepare to spread happy Mommy joy when I am with my kids. Not always possible, but I try.* —Sara

And we should all try to stay calm and focused. Kids should be allowed to be kids. They shouldn't have to deal with late mortgages, long work hours, or personal issues between their parents. Keeping this in mind, you'll become cognizant of the aura you emanate. When you're at peace and confident, so too is your family.

## Truth #3: YOU MUST DO WHAT WORKS BEST FOR YOUR FAMILY

You've read books, talked with your mother, sisters, and friends—all to get advice on how to be a good parent. Sometimes all that information can override your instincts and confuse you. As a mother you realize that you know what is best for your family. The trick is to take in all that advice, use what works for your family, and toss aside the rest.

## Truth #4: YOU GROW AS YOUR CHILDREN GROW

You grow into your mothering skills with each milestone your child reaches. Just as a woman who doesn't have children can't understand what it's really like to be a mother, you can't understand what it's like for a mom in another situation. You may empathize, but unless you have a child with a disability, you can't understand that mother's world. Until your child struggles with homework, you can't understand the pain that academic pressure can cause. Until you have a teenage daughter tell you "I hate you," you can't understand that mother's hurt.

## A MomsTown Tip
### ON ADOLESCENCE

> I finally came to terms with my daughter saying that she didn't like me and can be totally okay with that. Sometimes the decisions I made were not the most embraced. She'd get mad. I would drop her off at school; she would say she hated me and slam the door. I would tell her, "It's really okay if you don't like me. I love you, but rules are rules." It can be tough to stand your ground, but it's easier in the long run.—*Allison*

The great news about each stage of your child's growth is that you have an opportunity to grow as a mother and as a person. If you are the sum of your experiences, you have a lot of adding up left to do.

## Truth #5: YOU CAN'T DO IT ALL—CERTAINLY NOT ALL AT ONCE

You have to give up the notion of being all things to all people all at once. You can't possibly be Supermom, the super career woman, the woman with rock-hard abs, the hot babe in bed, and the public servant extraordinaire all at the same time. There will be times when things do run seamlessly, especially in one aspect of your life. But for you to expect that standard to be met on a daily basis is too much pressure.

# Truth #6: MOTHERS ARE HUMAN

We all make mistakes. Yes. That's true. You should ask yourself, "Did I learn a lesson?" If you can say yes, then you most likely won't make that particular mistake again. And hopefully, you've learned to show the same compassion to your children. We yell when we shouldn't yell. We have all spanked when we shouldn't have spanked. We've said things we shouldn't have said. We're parents yet we're still human. Do you want to put the screws to yourself to be perfect? Put the screws to your children to be perfect? Ridiculous! You've made mistakes and have past experiences you want to keep private and let go. To place the pressure on yourself to be perfect drains the joy and peace out of your daily life.

# Truth #7: KIDS ARE HUMAN TOO

They will have triumphs and failures. Accept that they are human too and will make mistakes. Remember mistakes are a good thing. How you handle mistakes shapes who you become and who your children become. Holding your children's hands when they need you and not judging them helps them to know they can trust you when they most need you. Sometimes your children need your love most when they least deserve it.

# Truth #8: ONE-ON-ONE MATTERS

Children feel special when you spend time with them on a one-on-one basis. There is excitement and there is more intense bonding. When you take this opportunity to spend time with them and listen to them, they know that they are important to you. One-on-one bonding can be as simple as cooking dinner together, going for an ice cream, or tossing a ball in the backyard. These special moments build confidence in your children, and you get the chance to know your child a little better.

## Truth #9: ACTION MEANS MORE THAN INTENTION

One of the greatest challenges moms deal with on a day-to-day basis is guilt. Guilt sneaks in when an action falls short of your intention. We'll address the differences between Good Guilt and Bad Guilt in a moment, but first let's realize that kids can only interpret what you do, not what you intend to do.

### A MomsTown Take on Guilt

*My husband and I finally agreed to downsize our home and living expenses so that I could cut back my hours at work. I got tired of the disappointment I saw in my boys' eyes when I would say, "Not now, later." After a while they took it as my way of saying no. Each time, I fully intended to play ball in the backyard with them "later," but it never seemed to happen when I was working long hours. Now I can spend the time with them that they deserve, and we are a much happier family. —Gail*

To act on your intentions, first be aware of what you want to do and what you're actually able to do. Start small and steady. Taking ten minutes to read a chapter in a book is easy and makes a huge impact on your kids. Then—here's the key—promise yourself before you promise them. The goal here is to build trust and confidence with your children. When you say you're going to do something, you want them to know you're going to follow through. And here's a beautiful thing: you won't feel guilty anymore.

# Truth #10: THEY'RE WATCHING US

Just as every mom has eyes in the back of her head, we believe kids have secret eyes too. They are watching and learning from you all the time, and they are taking mental notes. Moms are important role models. You teach your children to take care of themselves by taking care of yourself.

## A MomsTown Tip
### ABOUT GUILT IN THE MARINADE

> I recently bumped into a friend at the grocery store and asked her, "What's cooking at your house tonight?" She then began to outline her menu. She was buying a pork loin to marinate, salad fixings, and a vegetable. I responded, "You lost me at the marinade." She said she was creating an elaborate meal out of guilt because she was so busy with volunteer efforts at her son's school, her daughter's mounting homework, and the duties of running the household. Takeout and those meals quickly thrown together at the last minute were beginning to eat at her conscience. —Adella

Our girlfriend's guilt over the marinade got us thinking about one of the hot topics we talk about with moms: Good Guilt versus Bad Guilt. Let us begin by suggesting that if you find a way to eliminate guilt entirely from a mother's life, send us the million-dollar secret (we'll be more than happy to split the profits with you). For those of us who routinely deal with managing guilt, here's some encouraging news: there is such a thing as Good Guilt. Good Guilt is the kind of guilt that motivates you to make positive changes in your life. For example, guilt about eating takeout every night is good. That kind of Good Guilt drove our friend to marinating a pork loin and fixing salad for her family.

Other examples of Good Guilt are feeling antsy because you

haven't been working out at all. That kind of Good Guilt gets you into the gym, out to walk around the neighborhood, or into a yoga class. Good Guilt guides you in positive ways.

On the flip side, Bad Guilt diminishes your self-worth, drains your energy, and causes unnecessary anxiety. Bad Guilt sneaks in when you feel guilty about not volunteering for a committee at school when you're already committed to another one. Bad Guilt flares up when you just can't bring yourself to say no. This kind of guilt creates more anxiety in your world, causing you to be overwhelmed and making you spread yourself too thin.

## Bonus Truth: YOU ARE YOUR CHILD'S NUMBER ONE ADVOCATE

It is part of your job description to look out for the best interests of your children. You can't always rely on schools, teachers, and coaches to do it. Quite honestly, it's not their job. And the basic truth is no one loves your children the way you do.

Raising children is considerably different today than it was twenty or thirty years ago. For one thing, when you were a kid, kindergarten was all about painting on your dad's T-shirt and learning the alphabet. Kindergartners today are prepping for the competitive world of elementary school. They are logging the number of minutes they read after school and bringing in book reports. We often wonder why we allow this kind of pressure to be put on our kids. Are we *really* that afraid they won't succeed? Do we fear they'll be left to dig ditches while the gifted-and-talented child across the street grows up to run the world? Are we really raising leaders, creative thinkers, and healthy, well-adjusted people? Or are we on the path to raising a generation of high-blood-pressured, overstressed, honking, road-raging adults?

This question was posed to us by the owner of a public relations company based in Boston. Her company represents several household brands including LEGO. LEGO was preparing to host a media panel on the importance of creativity in the playroom and in the schoolroom. Laura at the public relations company asked us if we had an opinion on this issue or if we had talked to moms who do. Our answer was a resounding yes!

**We see imagination and creativity being sidelined in the pursuit of perfect grades.**

We traveled to New York to sit on the media panel. One of the panelists who captivated us was Mitch Resnick. He's the founder of MIT's Lifelong Kindergarten Lab. The purpose of the lab is to discover how children best learn. And wouldn't you know it, according to Resnick, kids learn best through creative play and teamwork, not sitting for hours in a classroom, listening to teachers drone on, and powering through endless repetitive worksheets. He says that unfortunately the academic trend is pushing kindergarten classrooms to become more like the upper grades, when the trend should be the exact opposite.

*My eldest son's greatest complaint when he went to first grade (and I remember it vividly) was that there was no more free time. I remember the pit in my stomach that for my son at the ripe old age of six, playtime was over. It was now time for my son to start fitting into the box. And I'll tell you, in all honesty, I put as much pressure on him as his first grade teacher to fit into that box. Reading at his pace, writing at his pace, and completing math sheets at his pace was not going to be acceptable. We were going to push. And push I did for the next two years, until it just hit me. This wasn't working. I changed course. I moved him into an environment that was self-paced, a Montessori school that believes children inherently want to learn, where worksheets are a part of the curriculum, not the curriculum; an environment where teachers believe in family time and not homework time. Wouldn't you know it; he scored well above average on the standardized test and in the third grade even scored post-high school in some areas. The greatest moment for me, however, was not the day we got the* test scores. It was the day of driving in the car and hearing him tell me, "You know what, Mom? I don't have headaches and tummy aches anymore." —Lisa

We recognize that moving a child to private school isn't a feasible plan for most families, and changing schools and even teachers is not always possible. As mothers, we all agree that we have the right to be active in our child's school, and our being proactive is in our child's best interest. We do strongly believe that our children don't and shouldn't be expected to all learn the same way. Children are as unique as their mothers.

We talk to moms every day who are worried about the pressure being put on their kids. We know what it's like to have a first grader who hasn't mastered chapter books in the second week of school and to have a teacher say, "I know you say he's bright, I just don't see it." We know what it's like to sit at the kitchen table for two hours each night while our children struggle through their tears to get their homework finished. We know what it's like to have a child who has chronic tummy aches and headaches and hates going to school. We know what it's like to have our child placed in a class with a teacher who is not a good fit for that child.

## A MomsTown Take on Teachers

My daughter suffered through fourth grade with a teacher she feared. She felt as though she couldn't please the teacher no matter how hard she tried. I left her in the class because I wanted to teach her the life lesson that you have to work with people you might not like. However, when we got to the fifth grade, there the teacher was again. She had been moved to teach the fifth grade and my daughter once again was in her class. This time I fought it and won. —Michelle

We all have to do what we think is best for our child at any given moment or in any given situation.

We hear from moms who wait up every Friday and Saturday night, praying that their child comes home safe from the high school football game. We're all afraid our kids will either drink and drive or get into a car with someone who is reckless. We know what it's like to worry about our kids every day. We worry not only about their physical safety but also about their emotional lives, their friendships, and their futures.

Worry is one of those parent feelings that simply never goes away. We have never heard of a good way to eliminate worry from a mom's life. Accept the reality that they will get their feelings hurt, possibly struggle in school, get cut from a team, and catch a cold. Those are the parts of life that help children grow stronger. When possible, keep an open line of communication with your child, spend time with your child, and trust your motherly instincts.

# PARENTS AS THE CULPRITS
## Over-the-Top Programming
While many of you feel that there is too much pressure at school, you should realize that there may be too much pressure at home as well.

> This is a crazy week. Both kids have soccer practice, Brit has Spanish and piano, and Trevor has swimming and guitar. I feel like all I do is drive from one practice, game, or lesson to another. —Suzanne

Suzanne spends most afternoons in her car; her kids spend most afternoons chasing their busy schedules. It's almost like there's an unspoken competition to see which family can squeeze the most stuff into one day. It's as if the more overscheduled you are, the more successful you will be. Personally, we'd like to be excluded from this game, and we know a lot of other moms who would too.

**Why do we feel the need to make sure our kids are never bored?**

Boredom can be a good thing. It forces kids to think for themselves, to be creative on their own, and to learn to enjoy free time. When every afternoon is structured, kids lose out on a lot. They become reactive, not proactive. Instead of using their imaginations to create a fun game or spending time on a hobby, they wait for the next round of scheduled activity.

> I remember when baseball was about a bunch of kids getting together on an empty lot, picking teams, and figuring out the rules together. Today, there are coaches and thirty parents yelling from the sidelines on what the kids should do next. Every move and every play is critiqued. —Julene

Think back to when you were pregnant. Were you thinking how great it was going to be to raise a competitive child? Were you thinking how great your life was going to be chasing your tail and running on empty? Were you thinking how great it was going to be to always be in a rush? No. Instead you were probably, like us, thinking about how beautiful and fulfilling life would be. You were probably thinking about the love and forecasting the cherished moments.

When we get in too big a hurry, with too many deadlines, and our families are running around with their hair on fire, we think back to the day when our belly was full of baby. We remind ourselves of the truly important things in life. This allows us to get perspective on our schedules and the quality of our family life. We limit our kids' activities and we limit our own outside responsibilities.

# LETTING THE KIDS RUN THE SHOW

In addition to overscheduling our families' lives, we moms often make the mistake of letting the kids think they rule the roost and any other roost they happen to be in.

> *We went to a restaurant on the wharf in Monterey. There was a sign that read, "If your child cries or acts up, you will be asked to leave." At first, I was offended that management assumed my children were going to be out of line. Then I remembered being at the bagel shop watching a mom with two young kids. She had one baby in a high chair and the other child was racing back and forth the length of the entire store. People in line were being forced to get out of the kid's way. The mom kept saying, "Jake, slow down." I remember thinking, Slow down? If it were me, I'd keep a role of duct tape in my diaper bag.* —Tracy

Of course, Tracy was kidding about the duct tape, but apparently kids acting up in public are a growing menace. We recently saw a sign at a coffee shop that read, "If your children misbehave, we'll give them an espresso and a free puppy." Mothers were standing in line with a death grip on their cherubs' arms.

But the signs beg the question, "Why is it necessary for shop managers to parent, and why are there entire blogs dedicated to this issue?" We think it's because moms have lost the look. We were laughing in the radio studio the other day because we both remember the look. It was that look our moms could fire our way that stopped us dead in our tracks. We didn't dare talk back. We were even afraid to look back for fear that her look would burn a hole right through us. So, how do we get that look?

# GETTING THE LOOK

- Our moms weren't afraid of public humiliation and we knew it. If we ran around a store, they'd drag us out by our bangs.
- Our mothers followed through on their threats. If they said they were going to spank us, they did. (Now, we're not advocating spanking, but we do know we should follow through. If we tell them they're in a time-out or that they're grounded and we don't follow through, they'll know we're not serious; mad, but not serious.)
- We let our kids know what kind of behavior is acceptable and why. We let them know they're going to get one warning look, and after that there will be consequences.
- You and your husband need to support each other. The look is worthless if your partner doesn't back you and, worse, gives the culprits ice cream.

Kids, no matter how old they are, want boundaries. Any pediatrician will tell you the same.

> I even had my daughter throw it back in my face that I was too lenient with her. When she went to college, she said she got into trouble in high school because I let her stay out late. —CeCe

The truth is you do the best you can. Keeping an open mind and finding support is an absolute necessity. And hone your look; it can be an effective communication tool. We are grateful to our mothers for having taught us their looks so that we might pass them along to our children.

We are also grateful that we have our girlfriends, radio callers, and the women at MomsTown who encourage and support us on a daily basis. We have learned that what works for the family next door isn't necessarily going to work for our kids or for us. We remind ourselves that as moms, we are the pulse of the family.

It is also imperative that as a mom, you nourish your soul and your self so that you can take care of your family. You will make mistakes, you will fail, but you will also have many triumphs. In your roles as mother and wife, make a pact to take care of yourself and to support other mothers. If you're in a grocery store and you see a mom having a particularly bad moment, let her know she's not alone. A warm smile, a pat on the back, or an offer to help will go a long way in making her feel better. After all, we're all moms, and we get it.

---

Call it a clan, call it a network, call it a tribe, call it a family. Whatever you call it, whoever you are, you need one.

—*Jane Howard, author of* Families

---

## Resources

Family First: Your Step-by-Step Plan for Creating a Phenomenal Family by Dr. Phil McGraw (Free Press, 2004). Several articles on this topic by Dr. Phil can also be found at www.drphil.com

Parent Effectiveness Training: The Proven Program for Raising Responsible Children by Thomas Gordon (Three Rivers Press, 2000). His website is www.gordontraining.com

No—Why Kids—of All Ages—Need to Hear It and Ways Parents Can Say It, by David Walsh, PhD (Free Press, 2007)

# Chapter 11

# "What's for Dinner?"

Tell me what you eat, I'll tell you who you are.
—Anthelme Brillat-Savarin

One of our favorite and most consuming topics is "What's for dinner?" It's the question with which every mom is all too familiar. You probably even remember asking your mom the same question when you were a kid. We do. But it's not the question that's the issue; it's the answer. Wouldn't it be nice to have your kids ask you what you're serving and have them respond with cheers and leaps of joy? Instead, too often when we tell our kids what's for dinner, we hear "Aghh," or even "Yuck, I hate that." So, we try to get away with Dino chicken, pizza, and grilled cheese, but then the dinner guilt starts to set in. Hard to believe, but as moms, we can even feel guilty about dinner.

**Food eats at moms every day.** We think about it, plan around it, and talk about it. Food frustrates and comforts us. Magazines glamorize it, television shows simplify and romanticize it. Every day reality hits us smack in the face at 7 a.m. We're pouring cereal into bowls and butter-ing toast all at the same time that we're packing lunches, but we have no clue what we're making for dinner. Doesn't sound glamorous, does it? But it does sound familiar.

We—Mary and Heather—are not chefs, our pantries could be a tad more organized, we'll never claim that we have dinner on the table *every* night, and heck, we don't even have our own cooking show. But we do have aprons that say, "Better Done than Perfect!" It's kind of our motto in life, and it's definitely our motto in the kitchen. Sometimes we make things out of boxes (think fluorescent orange cheese pack) and cans (think stuff that originally came out of a garden), and that's okay. We do, however, get the same anxiety that most moms get when they've run out of boxes and cans and have ordered takeout three nights running.

---

As a child, my family's menu consisted of two choices: take it or leave it.

—*Buddy Hackett*

---

We talk with moms at school and online every day, all of whom deal with the stress of "What's for dinner?" At the end of the day, we want our kids to have a healthy, well-rounded meal. We want to know that we're doing our best to nourish their little bodies and minds. We also want our husbands to be able to sit down to a hot meal, and once in a while, we ourselves would also like to actually sit down to dinner. However, the reality is that family life just seems to be a lot busier than it was when we were growing up, and getting the entire family to the dinner table at the same time is no easy task.

So, what's the answer? The answer is *Don't let dinnertime guilt eat at you.* In the following pages we've outlined some ideas to help you stream-line your kitchen, make grocery shopping easier, and make dinnertime and entertaining more fun. After all, food should be fun, not a chore.

The best way to eliminate guilt about dinnertime is to remember that only you can let yourself feel guilt. We hear from women who say it's just so much easier when their husbands are either late for dinner or pick something up for themselves on the way home from work. Women tell us the pressure to cook a full meal is gone when their husbands aren't home for dinner. In fact, we know a gal who says her husband is a real pressure cooker when it comes to dinner.

## A MomsTown Take on Dinner

I swear my husband, Joe, is living in the 1950s. He comes home from work every night and expects (no, let's say he demands) dinner on the table. He wants the table set; he wants soup or a salad, meat, potatoes, and at least one other side item. Then he always has to tell me how his mom used to have some kind of homemade dessert for after dinner. He's constantly raving about what a good cook and baker she was when they were kids. I can't tell you how many times I've bitten my lip to keep from telling him to go back and live with her. —Tanya

When Tanya sent us this MomsTown e-mail, we recommended that instead of biting her lip, she let her lips start flapping. We suggested she tell him that his constant raving about his mother's cooking hurt her feelings. It made Tanya feel inadequate in the kitchen and guilty that she wasn't doing enough for her husband and the kids. We also recommended that Tanya remind Joe that his mother didn't work full-time outside the home. Tanya works forty-plus hours a week at a law firm, yet she is still the only one in the house who feels compelled to get dinner on the table.

Wouldn't you agree it's a better strategy, if you were in Tanya's shoes, to let your husband know how you're feeling? Keeping it inside just builds resentment, and it's not a great marital or family strategy to start wishing your husband away from the dinner table.

## ATTITUDE IN THE KITCHEN

We know that a good attitude goes a long way in life, and a good attitude will serve you well in the kitchen too. If dinnertime ends the day on a sour note, then something needs to change. Ask for assistance. Tanya's husband seems to have stepped right out of a *Leave It to Beaver* episode. Well, her husband turned out not to be such a Neanderthal after all. She took our advice and talked to him—nicely. He had no idea his words were hurting her feelings, and he had no idea of the pressure she had been under. Joe now does the grocery shopping, and together they plan the dinner menus. He calls on his way home from the office to see if she needs anything from the store, and sometimes he volunteers to pick up a pizza!

> *All this time he thought I was just a type A kind of woman. Now that he pitches in and shares some of the load, I'm much happier at the end of the day. I'm even thinking about inviting his mom over to dinner!* —Tanya

Tanya's attitude changed because she asked for help. Not such a big deal, was it? We sometimes forget that we live in the twenty-first century. Roles have changed, and they have been changed for a long time. Husbands aren't shocked when their wives ask them to pitch in. But husbands aren't stupid, either. He'll let you run around with your hair on fire until the day you decide to put the fire out and light a fire under his *#@.

## WHY IS IT?

Why is it that we women work, take care of the bills, run the errands, clean the house, and are basically gone from the home just as long as our husbands, yet the majority of us are still the only ones cooking? For some reason, husbands really believe we can bring home the bacon and fry it up in the pan, while they take every night off. Now, we're not saying this is true of all husbands. We do know a few who know how to cook dinner, but a few are not enough. We'd love to come up with some kind of "Daddy's in the kitchen" campaign and let them feel the pressure of "What's for dinner?"

## TWO HEAD-SCRATCHERS ABOUT MEN AND COOKING

1. Why do men not hear the words to country songs?
2. Why do we have to cook every day?

Sometimes when we're driving with our husbands, listening to the country station, and tears are rolling down our face, they ask, "What's wrong?" We respond, "Did you not hear the song on the radio?" They say, "Yeah, I heard the music. I didn't hear what they were saying."

Well, the same thing goes for cooking. Just the way he enjoys the music, he enjoys dinner on the table every night, although he has no idea what we go through to get it there.

We have learned from the women on our forum and on our radio show that food is a major headache for them. But the good news is that all these moms have shared with us some really great dinnertime solutions.

## MomsTown Tips
### ON DINNERTIME

Once again, we would like to turn your attention to the fabulous moms at MomsTown. When we put out a call for dinnertime solutions, they responded with overwhelming enthusiasm.

> I sat down one day with a blank calendar page and wrote the whole month worth of dates in. Then I created a meal for every day and wrote it in the square. I listed the meat, the veggies, the

bread, and everything else right down to the desserts. It took some juggling, but I was able to do the whole month in about twenty minutes or less.

When I was done, I pinned it up right next to my kids' activity/regular calendar, and now everyone knows well in advance what I am making. When it comes time for grocery shopping, I look at the week ahead and only purchase what is required to make that meal, if I don't already have it on hand.

Here is the great part! I am no longer sitting around at 4:30 trying to decide what we are going to have for dinner. Now I just check the calendar in the morning and plan accordingly. If it is a Crock-Pot meal or baking or stovetop, I know when I need to start it and when it will be finished. —Phyllis

I found a neat website with a calendar that I use. It's especially great for families with kids in school. Not only does it help with meal planning, but it also helps me keep track of all the kids' after-school activities. The website is called www.MomAgenda.com. —Luci

A quick fix for days where the time has gotten away from me is to have a "light" dinner and have things that don't have to be cooked. Crackers, meat, pickles, and cheese, fruit, a loaf of fine bread and a glass of wine, salads, veggies and dip. I can get away with that every once in a while by saying the kids wanted it—not the wine (LOL). Actually it's a nice change sometimes. —Sara

I love the new dinner studio concept. You can make about 8–12 meals in one evening, bring them home, and freeze them. I put them in the fridge about 24–36 hours to defrost them before cooking. The cost is reasonable because I could make about 3–4 meals out of each preparation, since they serve 6. They even let you split them! —Alice

I definitely don't cook every night. We have way too many activities to be able to do that. When we do manage to sit down to eat dinner, whether it is leftovers or a fresh meal at home or if it is grabbing something out on our way to or from activities, I think it is such an important time to connect with the family. I have found that the meal preparation services that are available now are a huge help in managing the meal dilemma. —Barbara

"What's for dinner?" is on every woman's mind every day. So much so two moms decided to make a career out of it. They came to one of our Big Break parties. They wanted to start a business together. They had heard of an opportunity, but they weren't sure they were ready to jump into it. They found their courage and inspiration in talking with all the moms who didn't think their dream was crazy after all. About a week after the party they bought a Dream Dinners franchise.

Dream Dinners is a great concept. In two hours, you can walk into their shop, choose your preselected dinner menu, and assemble enough dinners to feed your family for a month. The ingredients are already measured; all you have to do is assemble the dinners. You put them in a foil pan, take them home, and put them in the freezer until you're ready to thaw them out and pop them in the oven. This business is such a success because it solves a universal problem: "What's for dinner?"

The Dinner A 'Fare, www.dinnerafare.com
My Girlfriend's Kitchen, www.mgfk.com
Let's Eat! www.letseatdinner.com
Main Dish Kitchen, http://maindishkitchen.com
Dream Dinners, www.dreamdinners.com
My Delicious Dinners, www.mydeliciousdinners.com
Super Suppers, www.supersuppers.com

## Dang-Near Quickies

1. Dang-near everything will go in a tortilla.
2. Dang-near anything will go in a Crock-Pot.
3. Dang-near nothing will please everyone.

Whoever invented the wrap, thanks. We can put breakfast in a tortilla (scrambled eggs, spinach, salsa) and we're on the road. Although we realize it's best to sit down and actually take ten to fifteen minutes to eat, sometimes the reality is we don't have the time. Just about anything short of a liquid can go in a tortilla, and you can get tortillas that are whole grain and made without lard.

Now, for the Crock-Pot, the slow cooker, the best appliance in the kitchen. Our hats are off to the inventor of this one. We'd also like to thank all the cooks out there for supplying us with great new recipes for the slow cooker. The Crock-Pot's not just for chuck roast anymore. There are so many ways to use this appliance year round. The best thing about it (and any slow-cooker convert will tell you the same) is how easy it is to use, how much time you'll save cooking, and how tasty things are when they come out. It's how Grandma used to cook, and it's dang good.

If you have any doubts about the slow cooker, consider Gracie Allen's classic recipe for roast beef:

One large roast of beef
One small roast of beef

Take the two roasts and put them in the oven. When the little one burns, the big one is done.

Finally, realize the absolute truth that dang-near nothing will please everyone; it takes the pressure off. Let's admit it, most of us know what it's like to cook two or three different meals every night so that our children don't go to bed hungry. We've done it: we've cooked a great piece of salmon, steamed some veggies, and even popped potatoes in the oven, only to have our kids turn their noses up at it. We then end up making mac 'n cheese or some other less healthy meal just to please them. The truth is, when you do this, you're not doing your kids any favors. In fact, you're making things worse for them.

Developing a taste for healthy foods can be difficult for your kids and for you. Many Americans are accustomed to eating prepackaged, sugary foods. Sure, you may leave the table feeling satisfied, but the diet is simply not good for you. We're sure you grew up and your parents grew up with the motto, "You'll eat what everyone else is eating." You're a busy mom; you simply don't have the time to cook (let alone cook multiple meals) every night. If, at first, it seems easier to avoid the meltdowns or the arguments, you have to remind yourself that parenting isn't always easy, even in the kitchen. Remember, dang-near nothing will please everyone. Stop banging your head against the oven trying to do the impossible.

## SHOPPING ON A BUDGET

The real money-saving work is done at the supermarket. The most obvious money-saving tip when going to the market is to use coupons and to frequent the stores that promote double-coupon savings. We all know that we should be using coupons. So, why is it so many of us don't? Why is it we clip them, and they end up left on the kitchen counter or in an envelope in our office or buried at the bottom of the junk drawer in our kitchen? Why do they sometimes not even make it out of the Sunday paper?

Consider investing in one of those handy plastic coupon holders that are divided by type of food product and other categories for the home. Carry those Sunday coupon sections with you with a pair of scissors. Keep the coupon holder in your purse, so that it is handy when you are heading for the supermarket. In one or two Quickie sessions, you will be amazed at how much money you can save!

## A MomsTown Confessional

> *Typically, I don't even begin to think about dinner until I'm in my car driving home from work. I make a couple of calls, one to my husband, who asks, "What-r-we-havin-for-dinner?" I respond, "Honey, you're breaking up." I quickly hang up the phone as if the call were dropped, flip a U-turn, and screech into the grocery store parking lot. I dash in, grabbing ready-made salad, one of those hot roasted chickens from the deli, a loaf of French bread, a gallon of milk, and a pint of his favorite ice cream to sweeten him up.*
> —Matty

## EIGHT WAYS TO SAVE WHEN BUYING GROCERIES

1. **Shop at farmers' markets.** Most towns have a farmers' market where you'll save a lot of money on fruits and vegetables. You'll also find other items such as tamales, pastas, and sauces. We love farmers' markets not only for the money savings but also for the inspiration. The fresh produce, flowers, and friendly faces make us feel great and want to rush home to toss a salad.

2. **Buy generic store brands.** They are great. Keep in mind that the most expensive brand-name items are shelved at chest level. To save money, kneel down or reach up.

3. **Shop alone.** Hello. We call that a mom's night out. Heather's three-year-old was frequently acting out in the grocery store so that she had to leave. The last time it happened, she handed her cart, full of groceries, over to one of the clerks and not-so-discreetly excused herself from the store (much to the

relief of the other shoppers). When she asked her pediatrician for some advice on how to avoid a repeat performance, he said, "Don't take the kids shopping."

---

The woman just ahead of you at the supermarket checkout has all the delectable groceries you didn't even know they carried.

—*Mignon McLaughlin*

---

4. **Avoid nongrocery items.** You'll generally find them at much lower prices in department stores and pharmacies.
5. **Buy marked-down meat or bread.** When the store marks down meat and bread that's ready to expire, buy it. Eat it that night or freeze.
6. **Use a calculator.** Adding everything up while shopping will prevent checkout shock.
7. **Shop early in the day.** You'll get through faster and typically spend less.
8. **Beware of mood shopping.** Fatigue = carbohydrates; Anger = crunchy junk food; Gloom = sweets. So, only shop when you're happy.

## OTHER BUDGET REMINDERS

- Buy in bulk, if you have storage.
- Shop with a list.
- Shop the perimeter of the store. Shopping this way will save you money because the cheapest and generally healthier items are typically on the outer edges of the store. The pricier items, which are the prepackaged meals, are found on the inner aisles.

It's bizarre that the produce manager is more important to my children's health than the pediatrician.

—*Meryl Streep*

# THE EVERYDAY KITCHEN

Now that you've saved a little money at the grocery store, look at ways you can save yourself some time in the kitchen. We've already talked about the slow cooker; it's one of our favorite kitchen helpers, but not every dinner can come out of the Crock-Pot. So what can you do to make life a bit more streamlined in the kitchen?

At MomsTown, we've been listening to professional organizers and real moms who share their solutions on efficiency. If you'll recall, in Chapter 4 we discussed the kitchen Control Panel. We realized the Control Panel concept would work well in the kitchen after going on a tour of an amazing dream kitchen. We called up some contractors who don't just build any ol' regular home; they build multimillion-dollar houses for the rich (and sometimes famous). We had an opportunity to tour one of their recent sites, which was built for a famous golfer and his family. Needless to say, the *estate* is amazing. The entire home is beautiful, but our hearts skipped a beat when we went into the kitchen. The wife in this home-building team designed the kitchen (and that was a brilliant move). She is a mom and she knew exactly how a kitchen should flow.

Before we tell you about her ideas, we want to point out that you don't need 1,500 square feet of kitchen to accomplish what she accomplished by spending hundreds of thousands of dollars in a state-of-the-art kitchen.

The first thing she created is a breakfast/after-school snack station. In the multimillion-dollar dream house, it has its own island, bar stools, a small cooktop, a mini fridge underneath, and cupboards and drawers for dishes and utensils. Her idea is that a mom could stand at that island and, without moving, have everthing she needed to make breakfast, prepare a snack, and chat with her kids the entire time.

For most of us, there is no mini fridge under the kitchen island. Heck, a lot of us probably don't even have an island in the kitchen. Our kitchens and our budgets just aren't that big. The solution is to think about what you do have in your kitchen. You have a refrigerator, cabinets, and drawers. Ideally, your cooktop is close to your fridge, but if not, that's okay. For starters, and for practical purposes, don't think about this cook station as a breakfast-only station. Think of it as your what-you-do-every-day-in-the-kitchen station. You cook the same way every day. You have a routine. And you have your Everyday Favorites. You use certain bowls, pots, pans, and utensils. You use a lot of the same ingredients and foods. Start thinking about your favorite tools in the kitchen and make a list of them.

Now, find a cupboard or two and a drawer or two near the stove and refrigerator. You can use these to relocate your Everyday Favorites. Your favorite pots, pans, baking sheets, bowls, and utensils will be put into this new Everyday Station. All of the other items that get used occasionally can be stored elsewhere. Keeping your Everyday Favorites close at hand will save you a lot of time in the kitchen.

Now, take a peek inside your fridge. Create a space on one shelf for everyday items, then do the same in the pantry. If you have cupboard space in your Everyday Station to move everyday dry goods from the pantry to the station, then that will also save time and make you more efficient in the kitchen.

The goal is to have just about everything you use on a daily basis close at hand or within a few steps. We've found it makes a huge difference when we're able to operate efficiently in the kitchen. This is not just about saving time or keeping you from darting from cupboard to drawer, to oven, to stove, to fridge, to sink. It's really about giving you a sense of calm and peace in the kitchen. After all, most of us are in the kitchen every day; being there should be an enjoyable experience every day, not an everyday frustration. And at MomsTown, we do everything within our ability to avoid frustration as much as possible; heaven knows there's enough of it we simply can't avoid, so we might as well make life easy when we can.

## Everyday Bonus Tip

- More than likely, you're not the only one in the house capable of unloading the dishwasher, setting the table, or cleaning up. Enlist the help of your husband and kids every day. Everyone works hard, and there's no reason why you should be the only one working a double shift. Remember that it's all in the phrasing and the communication. If you yell at your husband or kids, "Get in here and help!" they may do it, but they'll do it begrudgingly. Rather, try asking for help at a time when you're not frazzled or trying to get the dishes into the dishwasher after a long day. Ask them in a relaxed tone what they think they can do to help you out a bit more every day. You may be surprised to hear their answers.

## Cooking Tips from Our Moms at MomsTown

- No more tears. Unless you just need a good cry, when you're cutting onions, just run cold water over them as you peel them. The onions, not your eyes.
- To keep potatoes from sprouting, place an apple in the bag with the spuds.
- When frying potatoes, if you want them more golden brown, sprinkle them lightly with flour.

- Drop fresh celery leaves in the pot while cooking shrimp to get rid of the fishy smell.
- If you want to know if an egg is fresh, place it in a pan of cool, salted water. If it sinks, the egg is fresh; if it rises to the surface, toss it in the trash.
- Eggs will be fluffier if they are allowed to come to room temperature before beating.
- Hard-boiled eggs will peel easily when cracked and placed in cold water immediately after cooking. Or poke the egg with a small sewing needle before boiling, and the egg will peel easily.
- When panfrying, always heat the pan before adding the butter or oil.

## MomsTown Tips
### ON CHEATER MEALS

**LOs** These are the never-popular leftovers, which can sometimes be disguised enough for the kids but not Dad. LO side dishes are generally much more acceptable if you add a really nifty main dish.

---

The most remarkable thing about my mother is that for thirty years she served the family nothing but leftovers. The original meal has never been found.

—*Calvin Trillin*

---

**Eggs** Eggs can be used to create amazingly cheap, fast, and nutritious meals that work anytime. Breakfast you know about. Egg salads, egg sandwiches, and even omelettes are still fine for lunch. The real secret weapon is frittatas for dinner. (Or if you really get ambitious, soufflés!)

**MREs**  In the military, MREs are Meals Ready to Eat. They're dry, pasty, and mushy but edible. At MomsTown, MREs are Meals with Real Effort. MREs should be avoided at all times, except for special occasions. It's okay not to pour all your end-of-the-day energy into dinner. Our families would rather have us feeling good in the last hours before bedtime than stressed about a sink full of dirty pots and pans. MREs leave the kitchen looking like a war zone, and we don't want you to have to go through the battle every night.

**DAG**  This is a welcome sight and one that generally meets with the entire family's approval—Dad at the Grill. Naturally, you do the prep work while he heats up the outdoor oven. This should be quick, fairly easy, and even healthy if you give him some vegetables to grill too.

**EFTs**  (And we're not talking electronic funds transfer.) We're talking about Everyone Fending for Themselves. Occasionally even this one is okay in our book.

## THE MOMSTOWN SEASONED COOK

Cooking by the seasons and expanding your repertoire with the weather is the goal of the seasoned cook. Meals are constantly churning in the wheels of our minds. We have stored away in our meal memory a certain number of dinners that we cook at certain times of the year. They are effortless, made without a recipe or a cookbook.

However, we have found that an easier way to cook according to the season is to get four three-ring binders, one for each season. Label them Winter, Spring, Summer, and Fall. Put into each binder at least twelve recipes that you enjoy cooking for each particular season. Make sure these are easy recipes that don't require a lot of time to prepare. You can put as many recipes in the binder as you like, but we recommend not putting more than twenty-four in each season. The goal of the seasoned cook is to streamline the kitchen and to streamline the thinking that goes into meal preparation. Over the years, as you build your seasonal recipe repertoire, move old recipes to an archive. This can be one fat binder with all four seasons inside. If you feel superorganized, then have your recipes laminated or put them in a protective sheet before putting them in the binder. This will save them from spills and splashes.

---

As the days grow short, some faces grow long. But not mine. Every autumn, when the wind turns cold and darkness comes early, I am suddenly happy. It's time to start making soup again.

—*Leslie Newman*

---

Here are some examples of seasonal recipes that our families enjoy. We like to entertain and we are always looking for a new recipe to try. A great source of fun recipes is our friends. We also like the tried and true favorites our grandmothers passed down to us. Create your own family traditions and memories by cooking up wonderful meals to share with those you love.

# Winter: BEEF STEW

This classic comfort food is tough to beat. This is a great meal for a lazy Sunday. Start the stew and let it simmer while you take a much needed break from the week. This is easy to make and great for leftovers (if there are any!)

### Ingredients

2½ lbs. boneless, beef chuck roast, trimmed of fat

2 cups of white potatoes, peeled and cubed

6 carrots cut into chunks

1 white onion, chopped

1½ cups of beef broth

½ tsp. pepper

½ tsp. salt

1-15 oz can of corn

1-15 oz can of peas

### Steps

Brown meat in oil in a 12-inch skillet, about 15 minutes.

Transfer beef to stock pot.

Add 3 cups of hot water, salt, and pepper.

Heat to boiling and reduce to simmer for 2–2½ hours.

Add in potato, carrots, onion, and beef broth.

Cover and simmer until vegetables are tender, approximately 30 minutes.

Gently stir in corn and peas and prepare to serve.

---

Recipe: A series of step-by-step instructions for preparing ingredients you forgot to buy, in utensils you don't own, to make a dish the dog wouldn't eat.

—*Author unknown*

# Spring: CHICKEN KABOBS ON BED OF PINEAPPLE RICE

**Ingredients**

4 chicken breasts cut in large cubes

1 onion

2 bell peppers, green or red

1 bag (3½-ounce) boil-in-bag long-grain rice

2 tsp. butter

1 cup diced fresh pineapple

2 tbsp. fresh cilantro, chopped

¼ tsp. salt

**Steps**

Cut onion and bell peppers in large chunks.

Place chicken on skewers alternating with onions and bell peppers.

Grill for 10–15 minutes or until chicken juices run clear.

Cook rice and place rice in a large bowl.

In a nonstick skillet, melt butter over medium-high heat.

Add pineapple and sauté 4 minutes, or until pineapple begins to brown.

Add cooked pineapple, cilantro and ¼ teaspoon salt to rice in bowl.

Serve chicken skewers on top of bed of pineapple rice.

# Summer: ISLAND CHICKEN SALAD

This salad is a crowd pleaser. Refreshing and unique. You are sure to wow your guests when you serve this one at your next barbeque.

### Ingredients

2 chicken breasts, grilled and sliced into strips
¼ cup red wine vinegar
½ cup pineapple juice
1 shallot, minced
1½ cups canola oil
1 mango & 1 papaya, peeled seeded and cut into
¼-inch strips
½ cup dried apricots
½ cup golden raisins
½ cup macadamia nuts, chopped
6 cups mixed greens
Salt and pepper

### Steps

For dressing, combine vinegar, pineapple juice and shallot.
Slowly, whisk in canola oil and salt and pepper to taste.
In a mixing bowl, add mango, papaya, dried apricots, golden
    raisins, macadamia nuts and 1 cup of the vinaigrette.
Sprinkle with salt and pepper.
Place greens on a large platter or in a serving bowl and top with
    fruit mixture.
When ready to serve, top with chicken and remainder of dressing.

# Fall: TAMALE CASSEROLE

This hearty meal is sure to warm the autumn evenings. Be sure to start a fire and enjoy a nice cozy evening at home with a delicious meal.

### Ingredients

1½ lbs. ground beef
1 small onion
2 cloves of garlic, finely chopped
1-16 oz can enchilada sauce
1 cup whole kernel corn
1 can (2½ oz) sliced olives, drained
1 tsp. salt
2¼ cups yellow corn meal
1-12 oz can of evaporated milk
1-4 oz can diced green chiles
½ cup cheddar cheese shredded

### Steps

In a large skillet, cook beef with onion and garlic.

Add enchilada sauce, corn, olives and salt.

Preheat oven to 425°F and grease a 12 X 8-inch baking dish.

In a medium saucepan, mix corn meal, water, evaporated milk and salt.

Stir frequently over medium-high heat for 5–8 minutes (mixture should thicken).

Stir in chiles.

Take out 2 cups of mixture and set aside covered in plastic.

Empty remaining mixture from saucepan into baking dish.

Spread on bottom and up sides.

Bake for 10 minutes and let cool.

Fill with beef mixture and cover with remaining corn meal mixture.

Bake for 15–20 minutes.

Sprinkle with cheese and cook and additional 5–10 minutes until cheese is melted.

# WHO'S COMING TO DINNER?

Now that we've discussed "What's for dinner?" we want to take a look at "Who's coming to dinner?"

We all love a good party, but few of us love to throw a good party, and some of us don't even know what makes a good party. That's why when we have questions about entertaining for a small group or even a large group, we turn to the experts in entertaining. There is no doubt you can get some great tips by turning on the Food Network or even going to websites about how to entertain, but we have a friend who joins us on our radio show every now and then.

His name is Eddie Osterland. Eddie was the first master sommelier in the United States. We love having him as a guest on the MomsTown show because . . . why do you think? He brings wine, and once he even brought us a $35 can of tuna.

Here's what Eddie has to say: Always slightly chill reds. A great red wine tastes good because it has just the right amount of sweetness to balance its acidity. Slightly chilling red wine enhances its sweetness.

The ideal temperature for reds is between 65 and 68 degrees. For this reason you should chill reds in the fridge for about fifteen minutes before your guests arrive. Likewise, Eddie says you should take white wines out of the refrigerator fifteen minutes before your guests arrive. He says the biggest mistake most people make is serving whites too cold and reds too warm.

Eddie adds, "Our appetite is very fragile, which is to say that our sense of hunger quickly erodes once eating begins. The lesson to be learned here is that if you want to impress your guests, make sure to serve them the best first. The first thirty minutes is critical for impact. After that, people assume a *refueling mode*, rarely talking about the quality of what they are consuming."

# Eddie's Appetizer: PARMESAN TOASTS

This simple recipe has unbelievable impact when served with sparkling wines! Make a mixture of 60% grated parmesan cheese (the best you can buy) and 40% mayonnaise. To this, add grated black pepper, chopped garlic (1–2 cloves), and some chopped fresh parsley. Eddie sometimes adds a dash of cayenne to take it up one notch (it should be just slightly perceptible).

Create some sourdough toast rounds, pipe this mixture on top, and broil until golden brown. Serve hot!

For more great wine and entertaining tips from Eddie, go to www.eddieosterland.com.

# BON APPETIT

Life is good, food is good, and sharing them both with family and friends makes everything more delectable. Sure we realize that a family sit-down dinner every night may be tough to accomplish, especially with our busy lives and schedules, but let's all try to slow down just a bit, at least long enough to chew. Honestly, in our households, we try to sit down to dinner as a family three or four times a week. That seems reasonable for our families. The key is to find what works for you and your family. Like every person, every family is different. Every family has a different schedule and different needs. There's no need to keep up with Mrs. Jones in the kitchen.

With that said, we have learned that the dinner hour is a great opportunity to connect with our families. In the Twenty-first-Century Frenzy we discussed in "Hold Your Family Close," the time we can find to talk and actually look each other in the eye can be fleeting. The day rushes by so fast that we hardly have a moment to say hello before saying good night. Dinnertime can be a bonding time between you and your spouse and the children; sometimes you even get a chance to get to know more . . .

Our daughter's friends actually started showing up at our house for dinner. They loved that there was always a home-cooked meal on the table, but I think they came over for more than just the food. They loved to share their stories. We loved it too. We got to know her friends on a deeper level. Now that our daughter has gone off to college, I really miss those evenings of sitting around the table with all those girls. I really miss all of the giggling.
—Darla

Dinnertime is a time to be spent with family and friends. It truly is a time to cherish. The food and the conversation may make wonderful memories, but the connections that are made over a meal will last a lifetime.

# Chapter 12

# Mom and Ms. Success

You can have a great life and never achieve the elusive work/home balance. In reality, balance is a moving target—you keep aiming at hitting it, but it keeps moving—and the best thing you can do is to keep moving too. You can move throughout your day, modifying your schedule and reorganizing your responsibilities, in the attempt to make things run smoothly. But it is still difficult to merge Mom and Ms. Success.

We work outside the home and we know a lot of moms who do as well, and we hear a lot of blah, blah, blah on how to achieve career/family balance. Experts give us their philosophies on how to make it all work. Fact is, working full-time and raising kids is tough. There's no way around it. We feel guilty when we're not volunteering in our children's classroom, when we're not available for the all-day field trip, when we've ordered takeout for the third night in a row, when we have to work late and end up racing for the day care, hoping we're not the last one to pick up our child.

We're continually asking ourselves, "How do other working moms do it? Are they really achieving career/family balance?" We wonder if their husbands help out more with the household chores, or if they have someone else cleaning their house and running errands. We wonder if they ever send their kids to day care with runny noses. We wonder if they're struggling to pay the bills and balance the checkbook. We wonder if they ever forget appointments and worry about how their children are doing in school. Do they worry if their teenage daughter is having sex or if their son is going to host the kegger when they're out of town? Sometimes we feel as though our work is getting in the way of our having a real handle on our children and our lives. We say to ourselves, "If only I didn't work!" But lady, that's not the answer. Most of us are working for two reasons (and they're two really good reasons):

1. The family needs the paycheck.

> I work at a big bank in downtown Chicago. I work with a lot of
> other moms. I'm working because this is an expensive town to live
> in. I don't know how families make it on one income in this
> town. We need two, and two high ones to boot! —Jen

2. It's who you are. Your career is part of your identity. To give it
   up would be to give up a major part of yourself.

> I feel like being a working mom makes me a better mom. My kids
> see me following my own passion in life, and I believe that makes
> me a good role model. —Noel

So, then what is the answer? How do you get the work/home balance that we're all craving?

Here's a place to start: stop wondering how others do it. Really, who cares? What you should most be concerned about is how you are doing it. When you stop wrestling with the idea that you're failing in some way or that you're in some kind of funky competition with the family next door, then you can look at the real changes that need to be made.

The first thing to address is your job. Do you like it or is it the root of your discontent? If you like it, then it is worth discussing with your boss flextime options to help you meet family obligations and responsibilities. If, on the other hand, you hate your job, hate your boss, and dread waking up in the morning, you should reevaluate your work choice and start looking for another job. In fact, what you've got is a job, not a *career*, and you need to change.

> *The one tip I would give to any fellow single working mom is to be passionate about her work. It would be unbearable for me to have to go to work every day to a job I didn't love. It's hard enough to be a single working mom without hating my job.* —Lisa, kindergarten teacher, mom to four boys

**It's time to consider handing in the pink slip . . .**

- ☉ when you feel chronically sick and depressed.
- ☉ when you feel trapped, like there's no way out.
- ☉ when you feel like you've been pushed into a job that is almost insurmountable.
- ☉ when the money's fine, but there's no potential for advancement.

Assuming that you would like to continue doing what you're doing but under better conditions, let's look at how you can make some real changes to improve the quality of your everyday life.

## MomsTown Tips
### ON CAREER ISSUES

Again, we get our best ideas from the MomsTown moms:

**We want flexibility.** A flexible schedule is the greatest issue for most of us. And we want flexibility without having to give up "advance-ability."

> I'm a first-time mom. I gave birth in April and have to go back to work in six months. My company gave me a great maternity leave; however, it has abolished its program that allowed employees to work flex hours (which meant I could work four ten-hour days rather than five days a week). That extra day off to spend with my baby would be great. —Miranda

**We want mobility.** We want to be able to take our work out of the office.

> I love the idea of working part-time at the office and part-time at home. If I could be at home at least two days a week, that would make a huge difference for my family. —Jody

**We want trust.** We want our employers to trust that we are better employees when we have flexibility and mobility and that we won't take advantage of those privileges.

> I'm a grown woman and I've been with the same company for seven years. I'm a controller for a small home furnishings company. I know my responsibilities and what is expected of me. I also know that I would be happier being able to work part-time from home. If I could just convince the owner of the company to let me prove myself! —Tamara

**We want corporate family programs.** A lot of companies are waking up to the idea that on-site day care is a fabulous deal for both the working mom and the company. However, we realize the expense of this innovation is oftentimes too much for businesses to take on, especially small businesses. But when there are enough working parents at the same location with the same day care needs, companies might address this issue and offer a child care program for employees.

> I work for a publishing company. We have a lot of working parents. Actually, it's amazing how many nursing moms there are in this one building. What were we all doing a year ago? I have a pretty good idea! Anyway, our company set aside two office spaces with an outdoor patio as a day care. I can go anytime during the day to see my baby. I can't tell you the amount of stress it takes off me. It's really the reason I stayed in this job.
> —Lena

> My husband wants to hire a nanny; my mom thinks the baby should be in the same day care as my sister's children. I don't know what to do. I love my job and I don't want to quit, but the idea of dropping my baby off at 7:30 in the morning and not seeing her until 5:30 is truly making me sick. —Tricia

So what's preventing you from discussing these ideas with your employer? You know there are answers to your problems. The trouble most of us have is confessing to our bosses or coworkers what would help make us happier in our jobs and ultimately better employees.

## THIS IS FOR THE BOSS

To get the most out of us independent women, get REAL:

**Responsibility** Outline responsibilities, and together we can
build trust.

**Expectations** Give us clear, attainable expectations and timelines.

**Accountability** Schedule regular reviews, and then let us get to
work.

**Longevity** Realize that most of us are in it for the long haul.

> *I'm lucky I have a great boss. If my kids get sick, my boss is ex-*
> *tremely flexible. He's a dad and kids come first in his book. I don't*
> *know how I would do it otherwise. I know it's a struggle for other*
> *moms.* —Linda, single mom to two boys

There is an art to getting what you want: it's called negotiation.
Here are some negotiating tactics that have worked for us and for other
working moms we know.

## GETTING WHAT WE WANT AT WORK

1. Start with some negotiation at home. We have found that
   when we talk about what we need with our husbands, they
   can help us with some solutions. Perhaps your husband can
   also get some flextime at work so the two of you are working
   toward your family goals. When you ask your employer for
   help, you'll find, more often than not, that he or she is more
   than willing to help find a solution that makes everyone
   happier. But you have to ask.

2. Bosses want happy employees the same way husbands want
   happy wives, and children want happy mothers, and mothers
   want happy children and husbands. Employers are often

willing to be flexible with your hours; you just have to ask. Go into the boss's office with a suggested schedule of hours that better suits your lifestyle. Perhaps it's a compressed workweek with four ten-hour days, or it's coming in early to have the afternoon off.

3. It's always a smart move to determine your worth before you go into your boss's office. You'll be more apt to respond to his/her possible objections.

4. Remind yourself and your employer that you are more valuable when you're happier and that you are happier when you are able to be there for your children.

5. Don't worry about getting fired. Even the densest boss knows that it's going to cost them a lot more to replace you than to work out a mutually beneficial arrangement.

6. It is always smart to be assertive but not argumentative. Don't start any negotiation with "or else" tactics.

7. Do the math. How much are you willing to give up in the negotiation? Are you willing to take less money to get what you want? Sometimes benefits are a bargaining tool. Often women don't realize how much benefits cost employers and how willing they might be to negotiate these points.

8. Try to anticipate any objections or concerns you might run up against. Write them down along with your rebuttals.

9. Be very clear and communicate honestly. Don't try to paint a rosier picture for the benefit of your boss. Granted, you don't want to air your dirty laundry or unload your personal struggles; however, employers can't help you if they don't understand your situation.

10. Sometimes the employment shift is needed just for the short term. When you will be struggling for a defined period of time, try to negotiate a short-term solution. For example, our friend found out that her dad had cancer and needed a six-week course of radiation/chemotherapy treatment. Her

mom could no longer drive. Liz was the one who had to take him to the hospital for his 9 a.m. daily appointment. She negotiated with her boss to start work at noon. That temporary change worked for her boss, and it took some of the stress off an emotional and difficult situation.

## DARK CORNERS OF THE CAREER/FAMILY CONFLICT

So far, we've been discussing the most straightforward aspects of the conflicts most moms experience in trying to juggle family and career. However, our MomsTown correspondents point out that there are other aspects of the situation that can cause problems.

For example, career and family are two different and compartmentalized cultures. At work, Ms. Success is valued and often praised for her efforts and her knowledge. More important, the company expresses its appreciation for her in a very powerful way: cash. At home, Mom is often taken for granted—or worse yet, chastised for every departure from *Ozzie and Harriet* perfection. In some instances, husbands want a full-time mom and full control of the jointly earned finances. Somethin's gotta give.

Most moms agree that there is no comparison to the joy and the love of a good family situation, and many women feel that those rewards are more important than any raise or promotion at the office. On the other hand, it is nice to be reminded that you are special to your family on occasions other than Mother's Day. That's when date nights and Money Talks are invaluable, to remind Mom and Dad that they want and need each other. Dad needs to share financial decisions with his financial partner. (Gee, if the money issue was between two guys, there would be no problem!) Moreover, unless he's ready to pay the cook, laundress, babysitter, taxi driver, and personal sex slave in hard, cold American dollars, he had better remember that Dad owes Mom a lot of Psychic Income.

Most dads are terrible about Psychic Income. A few kind words, a hug, a compliment now and then—those simple gestures would go a long way. From what we hear in MomsTown, the best way to deal with this issue is head-on: remind your husband that Psychic Income is part of a good relationship. Do your part to set a good example in the same realm (most of us do already). Regularly sharing a few compliments makes for a much happier marriage.

There is another sensitive issue within the career/family conflict that most moms don't like to talk about. However, the MomsTown hotlines tell us it can be serious. In the competitive atmosphere of the office or the workplace, Ms. Success dresses for success. When women go to work outside the home, they put on attractive business attire and are more careful about their hair and their makeup. It only stands to reason: in most business situations, your first impression is your appearance. In contrast, mom often heads straight home from the gym and stays in her sweats. Who has time for makeup when you are scrubbing floors and hauling dirty laundry?

More troublesome is the fact that in the workplace, every woman is regarded as unattached, no matter how many rings she has on that finger. (In fairness, we should add that most men seem to feel less encumbered by marital vows when outside the possibility of any supervision.) Reality check: where do you think the extracurricular activities that fire up that 50 percent divorce rate start? Certainly not at the supermarket or the preschool, which are primarily populated by moms.

Don't get us wrong. There's nothing wrong with feeling that you are attractive or with getting admiring looks from the opposite sex. However, if there is a young working mom out there who has not been hit on at the office, we'd like to hear from her, because we hear from plenty of married women who get those not-so-subtle offers of a drink after work. Those offers are troublesome because sometimes they come from bosses, sometimes they are accompanied by inappropriate suggestions, and sometimes there are persistent admirers who won't take no for an answer.

In truth, in some secret part of their hearts, most women have to find the offer flattering. Equally true, however, is that the moment that you forget your family and you cross that line, you're heading for a marriage on the rocks. Worst of all, unless your admiring friend handles himself in a manner inappropriate enough to warrant charges of sexual harassment, you can't complain to your supervisor. And you certainly do not want to talk to your husband about it. Sadly, it becomes one more thing to feel guilty about.

## A MomsTown Tip
### ABOUT ADMIRERS

> The first couple of times men offered to buy me a drink or take me to dinner, I rebuffed them harshly and cried. But it has happened to me several times over the years, and I no longer feel angry or guilty about it. I know that my husband finds me sexy and attractive, so I guess it is not a surprise that other men do too. I am proud that I have the good sense to put my marriage first, and the men usually back off immediately when I say so. It doesn't bother me so much now when it happens periodically. In fact, I think I would begin to worry if other men didn't find me attractive.
> —JoAnne

# HOME AWAY FROM HOME
**Work is like having another family.**

Going to work is—from a social point of view—the inheritance of another family. You get the crazy aunt, the weird cousin, and even the micromanaging parent. We know you can choose your friends but you can't choose your family. The same could be said for your job and your coworkers. Sure, no one forces you to take a job or to stay in a job, but the truth is you're working because you need the job. Quitting is rarely an option. You have to try to stay related.

Relating to the people at work can be a whole other can of worms. We're going to share some job-related stories from our MomsTown moms.

> Work is my home away from home. There are some people here that I don't care for and others that I consider great friends. You can't pick your coworkers but you have to all get along. —Shelley

Elizabeth works for a growing technology company. She describes herself as driven but can't figure out why she keeps getting passed over for promotions. She goes to work every day, puts her nose to the grindstone, and does her job to the best of her ability, which means better than most. Technically speaking, Elizabeth deserves the advancement she desires. When we asked her about her coworkers, however, she knew nothing about them. She knew their names but that was pretty much it. She didn't have time for frivolous chats; in fact, it seemed like a huge waste of time to her. The barrier she created between herself and her coworkers may have cost her the promotion she had been wanting. A little effort put toward public relations goes a long way.

Conversely, Kimberly works in a bank. For a long time she has been working to get into management. She's a loan officer but she wasn't necessarily the best salesperson. She didn't have the highest sales numbers, but what she did have was the people skills. Every morning, she made a habit of walking from department to department saying hello, asking about kids, passing out compliments, and listening. She genuinely cared about her coworkers.

Kimberly moved up the ranks quickly. And she credits her success to her willingness to pat others on the back instead of using others' backs as a ladder for her to climb to the top.

You can't change your personality, but you can change the way you look at others. Coworkers have lives and family and friends who love them. You don't have to love them, but it is important to see them in that light. It's the best way to deal with a coworker you don't like. Be kind.

# CREATING A BETTER WORK ENVIRONMENT

Here are some ways to make life at work easier.

✓ Check for eyestrain: put your hand to your forehead in a salute. If your eyes feel relieved, your space is too bright. If you can't change the overhead lighting, bring a visor to work.

✓ Get a good desk chair and take the time to adjust it properly.

✓ Sit up straight. Good posture can change your mood immediately.

✓ Accessorize. Plants, pictures, even a small water feature are great for creating a more relaxing workspace. Just make sure you have ample room. Adding clutter to your workspace will make you crazy.

✓ Headsets are a must. There's nothing like keeping your hands free, and your neck won't get a crimp in it either.

✓ Keep healthy snacks readily available.

✓ Never say yes on the phone; instead, say, "I'll have to get back to you and let you know." We women are too quick to pile on the work and the stress. Give yourself time to consider if you truly have the time and the brain space to take on another commitment.

✓ Take care of difficult calls or e-mails as quickly as possible. Putting things off creates more stress. And who needs that?

✓ Go outside at least once a day, and if possible, take a walk. The sunlight and activity is good for your focus, mood, and retention of information.

✓Take five or ten. Quick breaks throughout the day help keep energy levels high.

✓Build friendships at work. Friends make everything more fun, even work.

✓Walk around the office and say hi to people in other departments.

✓If there is someone at work who has the effect of fingernails on a chalkboard on your nervous system, try this: say to yourself, "Walk in light." We got this little tip from Dr. Wayne Dyer in his book *Inspiration*. Whenever we are bugged at work, in line at the coffee shop, in traffic, we think, "Walk in light." Those three simple words can have a dramatic effect on your tolerance level.

One final note: working moms desperately seek ways to balance it all; otherwise they feel they are shortchanging their families and themselves. The key is to keep the priorities straight, and family will always win.

> *I have a flexible and understanding boss. If my sons have a sporting event, my boss will understand and forget if I leave work early that day. However, if I don't leave early and I miss their game, my sons will remember that forever.* —Deborah, single mom to two boys

## MomsTown Tips
### ON WORK/FAMILY BALANCE

**Make time to exercise.** Exercise keeps your energy level high, reduces your stress, and gives you a sense of control.

**Reserve one night a week for a date night.**

**Once a week, schedule one-on-one time with each child.**

Running errands with him or her doesn't count. Find an

activity you both can enjoy: it will build memories and
deepen your bonds.

**Create and keep a journal for each child.** Record your memories
of them at each age, what you experienced or felt that would
be special to them. You and your child will cherish these
journals.

**Enjoy your downtime with your family.** Even better, every night
for thirty minutes, sit in one room as a family and read, talk,
or do homework.

**Slow down.** Think of yourself as a calm woman, and you'll enjoy
more peace at home and at work. Be proud. You're a mother.

## Resources

Corporate Voices for Working Families, www.CVWorking
Families.org

National Association of Child Care Resources and Referral Agency,
www.NACCRRA.org

National Association for Female Executives, www.NAFE.com

*Chapter 13*

# The MomsTown
# Big Break

*Y*ou are creative. We've said it before, and we'll keep on saying it; as a woman you have within you the biological power to create life. Your creative juices keep flowing both before and after you become a mother. There's no sense in trying to hold them back. We hear from women across the globe who are absolutely bubbling over with creative ideas, and the majority of those ideas are related to starting a business and making money.

For whatever reason, you simply can't put the brakes on creativity, and the practical side is that you can't stop thinking of new ways to make money—especially from home. So, let's do something about it.

First, do you have a great idea for a business, an invention, a product, or a service? Do you know in your heart that if you had a chance to launch that business, it would be a success? Are you always on the lookout for that perfect home business idea? Or are you already in business but struggling to get to the next level? If so, you're probably wishing you could just get a break. Well, how about a Big Break?

We know what it's like to want, need, and deserve a break. We also know how it feels to turn dreams into reality. It's amazing. We want you to know that feeling too.

We hear from many women who have great ideas for business, but something is holding them back. It could be lack of time, money, confidence, support, or all four. If this sounds like you, then this is your lucky day. The MomsTown Big Break is all about helping busy women turn their ideas into dollars and make the money they've been dreaming of making.

---

If your energy is as boundless as your ambition, total commitment may be a way of life you should seriously consider.

—Dr. Joyce Brothers

---

You can go into business just to make money, but chances are you'll struggle, and it's a rare person who can really pull it off with great success. The person who can succeed in the long run is the person who is truly passionate about his or her ideas. We all want to make money, but our passion is not in the dollar. Passion is in your art, in your skills, in your talents, in your creativity, and in your drive to make a difference.

Think about the movie *Jerry Maguire*. The agent who stole Jerry's clients was in it just for the money. Jerry wanted to make a difference. He had a passion and a mission. He stuck to it and, in the end, made the money. The moral is that passion will lead you to profits. But let's be realistic; it's easy to say you're not in it for the money. Truth is, anyone in business who's not making money, after a while, will lose the passion. Spending time, resources, and energy on a business that doesn't pay you back monetarily is demoralizing.

We don't want that to happen to you. That's why we started the Big Break.

## WHAT'S THE BIG BREAK ALL ABOUT?

The MomsTown Big Break is by far the most popular segment of our radio show, and it's the most-visited place on our website. We started the MomsTown Big Break because we saw in moms a hunger for making money through their ideas. We also heard from thousands of women who had great ideas for businesses—ideas about which they were excited. We knew that we needed to find a way to help support them. In fact, it's become one of our passions: helping busy women turn their passions into profits—when possible, from the comfort of their own homes.

The MomsTown Big Break is popular because women inherently make great entrepreneurs. It's those sparks of creativity that get ignited deep in our souls. Once that spark of creativity has flared, there is an inner drive to keep it burning.

We at MomsTown see, hear, and read about this spark every day. We visit moms in business, moms call in to our radio show, and they send us e-mails. However, we've come to realize that the spark alone is simply not enough to make a profitable business. We also see the problems moms continually run into. We see them so clearly because we have made the same mistakes. After all, MomsTown isn't some overnight success. We've made some really bad business decisions, wasted thousands of dollars we couldn't afford to lose, and caused ourselves a lot of unnecessary stress along the way.

# MISTAKES WE MADE

**Spent too much money, too soon.** We spent too much money on a custom logo, custom website design, custom letterhead, business cards, and envelopes in the first flush. Be absolutely sure of your brand first.

**Hired independent contractors on a monthly retainer instead of paying by the hour.** Take it slow.

**Spent too much money on attorneys.** Know their fee and the time increments they base their charges on. Watch the clock while on the phone with an attorney, and note that they charge for e-mails too.

**Trusted others too quickly.** Don't automatically believe promises made.

**Hired or went into partnership with others too quickly.** It takes time to develop trust and compatibility in a relationship.

**Overpaid for services to be nice and didn't question invoices.** It's okay to question charges and to negotiate better rates and terms. It's just business, not personal.

**Signed contracts too quickly without negotiating terms.** We were afraid we would miss the opportunity to get into a contract and thought if we challenged deal points, the other party wouldn't want to do business with us. Again, it's just business. Negotiate. There's one thing worse than not getting a contract, and that is signing a bad one.

**Didn't have a long-term game plan for the business.** It's great to wing it, but if you don't know where you want to go, you're not working smart.

**Didn't set daily, weekly, and monthly monetary goals.** We thought if we built it, the money would come. Stupid. We have goals now. Entrepreneurs don't get a corporate paycheck every two weeks until they earn it themselves.

We started sharing with women the mistakes and the smart moves we've made. They're the kind of moves that got us our first radio show, brought us a six-figure book deal, and got our business featured on the Dr. Phil show. We now have "people" who are helping us in business, and some extract money from us on a daily basis. Needless to say, these people are older than six and eat more than Cheerios for breakfast.

We decided to call the segment the MomsTown Big Break because women have a lot of great ideas, but they just need a break. That break could be advice on how to get the most out of the little time they have during the day. It could be ideas on how to start with a shoestring of a budget; how to market and get the word out about their businesses; how to find resources; or simply how to find the inspiration, motivation, and support they need.

The MomsTown Big Break is not just a day at the spa or a fifteen-minute soak in the tub. It's a life-changing, inspiring, soul-soaring, in-the-trenches, boot-strapping kind of break—the kind of break that makes us excited to get up in the morning and too excited to go to sleep at night. It's helping women gain financial independence while doing what they love. The MomsTown Big Break gives women encouragement, inspiration, practical resources, and a plan of action.

# IS MY IDEA RIGHT FOR THE BIG BREAK?

We get this question a lot. Women want to know if they can be a part of the MomsTown Big Break. Our answer is always yes. We have helped women around the globe start businesses of all kinds and take their ventures to another level.

We started the MomsTown Big Break with four moms. In four weeks we decided we were going to help them launch their ideas into a real business.

We have learned a great deal through the process of guiding and encouraging these women to take sometimes scary steps toward success. You can take those steps too. They aren't for the faint of heart, but we believe you are capable of taking your crazy dream and making it a reality.

There are five parts to our method:

- Identify your dream—crazy as it may sound.
- Develop your strategy—and think big.
- Execute your plan—with lots of hard work.
- Measure your progress toward success—and celebrate as you succeed.
- And don't forget the Big Break step-by-step manual.

## WILD ABOUT BUSINESS

As a wildlife artist, Alison Seda found success in galleries. And when her second son was born, she knew she had to find a way to blend her art with her greatest inspiration, her children. She says her two boys share her love of the natural world, and this new side of her business allows the family to be involved.

She turned to the MomsTown Big Break, and within thirty days of some hard work, she was able find a T-shirt wholesaler to work with and a commercial silk screener to get her designs onto the shirts. She got Lil' Beastees into a boutique, launched a website and an online store, and began taking orders.

She says it hasn't been easy starting a new business. It has been expensive, it has taken a lot of time, and there have been growing pains. As with all developing businesses, there will be more, but she says simply, "I'm doing what I love with who I love." To learn more about Alison's line of children's clothing, go to www.SedaInk.com.

Cecilia, mother of two boys, is a teacher of Spanish. She has a passion for her language and heritage. She had been teaching Spanish to kids at her sons' school and decided that she was ready to take her passion to the next level. Feeling a bit overwhelmed by the prospect of taking her Spanish course to the online market, Cecilia contacted MomsTown. In less than an hour after a show, we got an e-mail from a mom in Miami who wanted to enroll in Cecilia's course. We also got an e-mail from another woman who had a great resource for Cecilia. And today our Spanish-speaking guru mom is running her own home-based business. We have no doubt she will fulfill her dream.

Here's what Cecilia accomplished in just thirty days with the Big Break:

1. Took the grain of an idea—teaching Spanish online—and transformed it into a workable concept.
2. Created the basis for an online curriculum that will enable intermediate Spanish students to pursue their goal of reviewing, polishing, and supplementing their language skills.
3. Selected a name for her website: eSpanishClass.com
4. Wrote the text for a website.
5. Created a living, breathing website that people can return to again and again as a source of education, knowledge, and enjoyment.
6. Began creating a series of lessons and assignments, the first of which can be viewed on her website.
7. Overcame her fear of public speaking and made four appearances on the MomsTown radio program to discuss and promote her website.
8. Began signing up students for her online Spanish courses.
9. Learned to push herself yet knew her limitations as she juggled family and home along with her online venture.
10. Launched a home-based business that will enable her to pursue her teaching career, earn income, and still be available as a wife and mom to her family.

Look at the potential! Look at the personal growth! Look at the accomplishments! No matter how you want to define it, Cecilia is a success!

## A BIG BREAK IN INTERIOR DESIGN

We want to talk about two other moms, Judy and Lyssa, who have also launched a successful business thanks to the MomsTown Big Break. They call it SpaceLift: isn't that a great name for an interior design business? We love it, and we love what these two very entrepreneurial stay-at-home moms were able to achieve in just thirty days:

1. After discussing the possibility for two years, they finally decided to go for it. They started to organize their thoughts about the business and really look at it as more than just a hobby. They launched SpaceLift Interior Redesign and Home Staging.

2. To save money, they created their very own website.

3. They overcame the intimidation and fear of rejection that comes with talking to complete strangers about their business and services.

4. They met with several Realtors to establish relationships for more jobs and made two presentations at Realtor offices. (Those were scary!)

5. They knew that unless they worked hard at getting the business off the ground quickly, they would never make it happen. Almost every Wednesday and Sunday, they went to broker's open and Sunday open houses to meet with Realtors and give them business cards and information. Several of those contacts turned into bids and jobs.

6. They attended chambers of commerce meetings for net-working opportunities and made several excellent contacts.

7. They decided to invest $2,500 each to purchase furniture and

other decorating items for their staging inventory. (This was scary for their husbands, but the moms loved it because it meant going shopping.)

8. They opened a business bank account and applied for a business credit card that offers cash-back bonuses.

9. They made five scary phone calls. They continue to make those phone calls because now they're not so scary.

10. They had a brilliant idea of the day—establishing cooperative relationships with a painter and housecleaner to exchange referrals.

11. They completed their media kit and e-mailed it to local media for a possible news story on their business.

12. And now here they are. After just thirty days in business, their phones started ringing off the hook!

## A MANUAL AND A NETWORK

The day we announced the mission of the MomsTown Big Break, we were inundated with e-mails and phone calls from women excited about the possibility of getting their own break in business. As a result, we created *The MomsTown Big Break Manual*. We quickly realized we were just two people, and if we were going to really help, we needed to provide women with materials, resources, and a network of contacts. All of which can now be found on our website. We invite you to come pay us and the other Big Break women a visit.

In the meantime, here's a sampling of women—and their businesses—who find inspiration, practical tips, networking, and exposure through the MomsTown Big Break:

Jennifer at DealTaker.com
Janice at InCaseOfEmergency.com
Jennifer at FamilyPaws.com
Jen at Make-Better-Choices.com

Annabelle at Annabellesboutique.com

Tammy at WAHPromotion.com

Annette at FunOnTheArk.com

Tina at DoReMeandYou.com

Danielle at ReflectionsofYou.com

Kimberly at SelfIndulgence.biz

Sue at WhatsCookingMama.com

Cindy at HomeGrownBabyStore.com

Shirin at ShirinStudio.com

Monica at CultureRevolution.tv

Pam at BracesCookbook.com

Tawra at LivingOnADime.com

Traci at AccountableKids.com

Jennifer at JenerationsBaby.com

Diana at SpaGirlParties.com

Shannon at ConnectionCreators.com

Evie at MommysLittleMonkey.com

Susan at KidsWealth.com

Heather at SmartMama.com

Laura at ShimmerStudio.com

Carol at SpiritualJourneys.biz

Carrie at OrganicallyGrownKids.com

Henriette at MeBodyandBath.com

Germaine at ScrapbookArtistry.com

Shannon at BigLakeSpa.com

Lynn at AManIsNotaPlan.com

China at RenaudNaturals.com

Jamie at JamiesPND.com

Jodi at PrettyMeBeads.com

Jill at GaksSnacks.com

Laura at BabySwap.net

Jodi at ParenttoParent.com

Elizabeth at CraftyGiftCreations.com

Margaret at AMillionWishes.com

Stephanie at ExpressiveFortunes.com

Rhonda at ComputerLandCentral.com

Jennifer at JennifersJournals.com

Chris at VenemaGraphics.com

Laurie at WorkWisely.net

Heike at Heikeonline.com

Barb at FeelsLikeMagic.com

Tiffany at LivingOnPurposeCoaching.com

Phyllis at BabySwags.com

ChristieLynn at HappyHambones.com

To continue this MomsTown list, we would need another book, but you get the picture. There are lots of creative women working in a lot of creative businesses from home. If you can picture your name on this list, you need to get involved in the MomsTown Big Break now.

## WHAT'S *YOUR* INCENTIVE?

There are two main reasons that motivate moms to want to make money. The first is that we need it. It's okay to want to pay the bills and have extra cash left over. The second is that moms want flexibility and freedom. We want the flexibility to control our schedule. We want to be with our children when they need us, to care for an aging parent, or to do something for ourselves. We want the flexibility to be able to run errands when we need to, schedule appointments, and not worry that we're running on someone else's clock. Flexibility gives us the time; freedom gives us the space. With freedom we are able to act on our potential, be creative, and live beyond the confines of the traditional workplace.

## LET MOMS BE YOUR MUSE

There is no doubt that you can find inspiration all around you. We have found that the best way to get a daily dose of inspired thinking, dreaming, and action is to get together with other like-minded women. At MomsTown you can find that community online and possibly in your home town. Our forum is active with women who are working on their Big Breaks. Our town chapters are providing local support to Big Breakers. Truth is moms enjoy talking about the kids, our relationships, and sharing the latest beauty tips, but when it comes right down to it, we're all looking for ways to balance our home life and balance our checkbook.

---

I have yet to hear a man ask for advice on how to combine marriage and a career.

—*Gloria Steinem*

---

## LET THEIR SUCCESS INSPIRE YOU

### Lisa Druxman, founder of StrollerStrides

Lisa Druxman is a mother of two. She is also the brains and the brawn behind a successful home-based business. Lisa has been in the fitness industry since 1990, but it wasn't until she became a mom that she realized the need for specialty "mom" fitness. As soon as Lisa's son was born, she got outside with her stroller. Not having the time to get back to the gym, she created a series of exercises to get herself back in shape. Before she knew it, a new workout was born. She started teaching other women how to get fit while pushing their children in a stroller. Through a lot of work, borrowed money, and lessons learned, Lisa has built a local fitness program for moms into a chain of franchises across the United States. To learn more, go to www.StrollerStrides.com.

## Adena Surabian, founder of Nature's Baby Products, Inc.

Adena, the mother of two girls, started a line of botanical hair and skin-care products after her daughter had a mysterious skin rash. Ultimately, she discovered that the culprit was a sunscreen. "I developed this product because I couldn't imagine putting chemicals on my babies' delicate hair and skin," says Adena.

On running a business, Adena echoes the experience of many mom entrepreneurs that running a business is not easy and there are a lot of misconceptions.

---

With growth comes more expenses. We're now in 600 stores, with 42 reps, and we just went international in Asia. On top of working, I take care of our children: taking them to school, grocery shopping, making dinner, doing laundry, etc., and I'm still working 16-hour days.

—*Adena Surabian*

---

For more information about Adena and her products, go to www.Naturesbabyproducts.com.

## Lisa Hammond, owner of Femail Creations

Femail Creations was born out of a passion to make a difference in the lives of women and girls. At the time the seeds of Lisa's dream were first planted, she was managing a construction company.

Creating a catalog seemed like the perfect chance to combine my creative side with my passion for women's issues. I didn't want to let the fact that I had absolutely no experience in the cataloging field stop me—and it hasn't! I have found that the best experience has been years of being a catalog shopper.

—*Lisa Hammond*

Being a catalog fiend, she often wished a woman-owned catalog would show up in her mailbox that she could support with her shopping dollars. When that catalog never came, she decided to create it herself. The process has been completely overwhelming at times and has required more courage than she ever imagined. Many late nights and long hours have gone into this dream. All of the positive letters, touching stories, and great feedback from the customers and artists kept her going.

Focusing support on women artists and women-owned businesses is the essence of Femail Creations. For more information visit www.femailcreations.com.

## Michelle Baratta, owner of MBatHome.com

Michelle's story has very humble beginnings: she started her company in her mom's living room while still in college.

She has a degree in fashion design and has studied art but always knew she wanted to own her own business, so she went on to business school. However, it was while she was working in a clothing store that everything changed.

> I started making jewelry for myself of hand-blown glass beads and silver wire. Customers kept asking me about my jewelry, so the owners asked me to make some pieces to sell in the store. It was an unexpected and immediate success!
>
> —*Michelle Baratta*

She then attended the Los Angeles Gift Show, and before she knew it, her designs were in forty stores and catalogs. Her jewelry has been seen on some of our favorite celebrities on television and film, such as Courtney Cox, Jennie Garth, Lisa Kudrow, and Meg Ryan, to name a few.

Michelle's company line is now a direct sales company, and she has more than 500 consultants. For more information about Michelle and her company, go to www.MBatHome.com.

\* \* \*

The statistics are undeniable; today more moms are starting businesses than ever before. That's why the MomsTown Big Break has not only been a breath of fresh air in the online community, but has also filled a growing need. That need is to have one place to find resources and support for the entrepreneurial mom. Our Big Break moms find the confidence to follow their dreams.

Now let's find the job that fulfills your creative side, that allows you to call the shots, be your own boss, have the flexibility you need, and have the potential of making a heck of a lot of coin.

# WHAT'S *YOUR* DREAM JOB?

The MomsTown Big Break helps women to identify their dream jobs. There are five key steps in finding the right pursuit:

1. **Identify the Natural You.** This is getting to the essence of your identity. The Natural You has talents that come easily. One way to identify the Natural You is to look back to when you were a young girl. What did you love to do? Were you a dancer? Did you play music? Did you love animals? Were you a tomboy or into any kind of sport? Did you find yourself absorbed in books, or did you love to go places? Did you love having things organized? Did you love researching and learning new things? Did you love nature? Were you driven to help others?

2. **Find what it is you love to do.** Write down a list of all your childhood hobbies. If you're having trouble remembering (because when you're a mom, sometimes memory is in short supply), ask your mom, dad, or siblings what you loved as a child. When we went in search of our natural selves, we found that we've always loved to talk and to write. We like to talk to each other, and we like to talk to other people as well. We like to write about our experiences and other people's experiences.

3. **Be true to and passionate about the Natural You.** Listen to your intuition.

---

Nobody can give you wiser advice than yourself.

—*Cicero*

---

4. **Journal it all.** Start writing. We can't tell you how many times we've gone back to the beginning, back to our initial writings. We have a small library of composition books, easel pads, and Microsoft Word files. Within our library are hundreds of hours of ideas, quickly or painstakingly jotted down. If it wasn't for our journaling, this book might never have happened.

---

By recording your dreams and goals on paper, you set in motion the process of becoming the person you most want to be. Put your future in good hands—your own.

—*Mark Victor Hansen*

---

5. **Don't wait.** Start today by removing any obstacles that stand in your way. The first obstacle might be uncertainty—doubting your own belief in yourself or your ideas. Don't let negative self-talk and pessimism stand between you and your dream job. If money, time, and others are standing in your way, then start finding ways to carve out the time, convince others of your idea, and the money will come. But you have to do more than just believe that your idea will be profitable. You have to start taking action. Today.

Answer the following questions to get a handle on where you are in your life right now in regard to starting or growing a home-based business:

**Do you have an idea for a business that makes you so excited you can barely sleep?** If so, you are one lucky person! If you have an original idea for a business you are passionate about, that's at least half the battle.

**Do you have an entrepreneurial spirit, or do you prefer to have someone tell you what to do?** This is an important question to ask yourself, because it will be entirely up to you to develop projects, organize your time, and follow through on details. Trust us; there will be a ton of details.

**How willing are you to get along with a variety of personalities?** You are the chief cook, bottle washer, and hostess. It is imperative to learn communication, etiquette, and conflict resolution skills to best handle clients, vendors, staff, and professionals, such as lawyers, accountants, and bankers.

**Do you have the physical and emotional stamina required to run a business?** Can you stand working every day on your business, possibly up to twelve hours each day?

**Can you weave your business into your day?** For example, are you able to be interrupted six to eight times an hour and still get something done? If your business is your passion, you probably won't have a problem with that. The key is to make sure you love what you're doing. (Of course, this does not mean you'll love every aspect of the administrative tasks or details, but the overall business should be your passion.)

**How decisive are you?** Can you make simple and critical decisions on the spot? And we mean on the spot! There will be opportunities and crises almost every day, and your ability to be discerning is crucial.

**How organized are you?** This is a tough one for many creative and passionate sorts. It is important to keep regular and accurate financial records and an up-to-date customer and vendor list. You must have a scheduling system that works for you. If you don't like having to be organized, you're going to struggle in your business.

And finally . . . when you're developing a successful business strategy, it is imperative to remember that it's all about you. The overall success of your business is *you*. It is imperative that you take time today and write down your personal mission statement. Answer the following questions:

What are my personal goals?
What are my business goals?
What are my strengths?
What are my weaknesses?
What am I willing to sacrifice?
What am I hoping to gain?

When you really take the time to answer the preceding questions, you'll be grateful to yourself for doing so. Your future as an entrepreneur will begin to crystallize.

## BRING IT HOME

Part of realizing your power is confronting your roadblocks—and the last place you might expect a roadblock is in the person sitting on your couch. Even though you have great intentions of helping out the family coffers, sometimes husbands or boyfriends may not be as enthusiastic. It's possible for your significant other to love and support you but not fully understand the vision you have to start and grow a business. And it won't just be a husband who might not get it. Friends, potential customers, mentors, and banks can't always see your vision. Therefore, you need a business plan.

# THE BUSINESS PLAN STARTS AT HOME

For starters, you are going to need a business plan to show your husband. We give you forms for a solid business plan that you can take to your hubby and to the bank. You'll find a business plan outline on our website at MomsTown.com.

Realize that your business plan is organic; it's a living document. It will change. If it doesn't, then your ideas are not evolving. It's also important to involve your husband in the process and to keep him abreast of the changes with regular updates. That will accomplish three things:

1. He will recognize that you are not afraid to talk to him about the setbacks, successes, dreams, and realities of your business.
2. It will prevent his getting anxious and having to approach you to find out how things are going. Trust us, the guys get anxious.
3. He could turn out to be a great business partner. We know a lot of men who have quit their day jobs to support a wife's endeavor, thus making it a family affair.

Also included in your plan should be the answers to the following questions:

- How do you plan to juggle the time you spend on your business with the responsibilities of being a wife and a mother?
- How do you plan to finance the start of your business?
- Are you going to borrow money from the family or apply for a loan?
- How much money do you need to get started?
- How do you plan to grow your business?
- Who and where are your customers?

- How are you going to market your product or service to them?
- How much time will pass before you make any money?
- How big do you want your business to grow, and what is the payoff?
- Why are you doing this, and how will you know when you've reached your goal?

Thoughtful answers to these questions are a good start to exploring the reality of how you're going to operate this business. Use the questions to help establish open communication with your husband, as well as to set expectations for yourself and get you ready to draft your working business plan.

## DEFINING THE BUSINESS IDEA

Once we have an idea for a business, we need to be clear about what the business is:

1. Is it a product, service, Internet, retail, distribution, or manufacturing business?
2. What industry does it belong to?
3. How did you get the idea?
4. What need does it fill?
5. What product or service will you sell?
6. Why do you think there is a market for your product or service?
7. How big do you want your business to be one day?
8. If you've already started your business, what are you stuck on? Are you struggling financially or having difficulty getting publicity and exposure for your business, or are you at a plateau and need to break through to the next level of growth?

In starting a business, there are no guarantees. There is no way to eliminate the risks, and they are not for the timid. It takes a lot of time, energy, and creativity to start a business. But if you have an idea you can't let go of, and you are willing to work hard and put a lot of passionate energy behind it, then you have a great shot.

You need to take time to do what is necessary to support and grow your passion, along with your regular day-to-day tasks, chores, and family demands. Staying at your best so you can work later into the evening or get up earlier in the morning takes energy. Good nutrition and exercise will help keep your mind sharp.

* * *

Now for the disclaimer: according to the U.S. Small Business Administration, over 50 percent of small businesses fail in the first year. We know there are many reasons that businesses fail. These can range from starting the wrong business at the wrong time to a family health or financial crisis to moving to other economic issues and the like.

---

No pessimist ever discovered the secrets of the stars, or sailed to an uncharted land, or opened a new heaven to the human spirit.

—Helen Keller

---

Also, keep in mind that businesses morph and change. Most entrepreneurs aren't in the original business they started. In fact we know several serial entrepreneurs. They just can't stop starting businesses.

In any new venture, there will be minor failures at marketing attempts or glitches when you pitch your product or service to a potential client. That's to be expected as part of the growing pains of a business. Try not to get discouraged if things are not going well and you have to shift gears. Often you'll be pleased with the end result. If something does not work that you thought would, just brush it off and try something else.

The main reason we share this reality is to highlight the importance of supporting one another and finding a network of support. Whether it's through MomsTown, a friend, or the local chamber of commerce, support is critical for anyone starting or running a business.

## GOING FOR IT

A lot of women get intimidated even asking for what they want, let alone going after what they want. This is where our MomsTown Big Break community of support will help bolster your confidence. And this is where the Unique You has to stand up and speak for herself.

We applaud the courage needed to take a stand and to tell the world you're going into business for yourself. Being an entrepreneur is an exciting yet risky proposition. No one can predict the outcome of even the most passionate, well-planned business. But all great entrepreneurs do the best they can and keep on trying.

We strongly encourage you to recognize that going for it doesn't just mean opening your doors and taking orders. When you go for it, be on the lookout. Always know your competition, know your customers, and know yourself. And just when you think you do know yourself, dig a little deeper, stretch a little further, and reach a little higher. You'll be amazed!

---

In design you have to love what you're doing first. If you don't love what you're doing, you can never come up with some good designs.

—*Jimmy Choo*

---

# STAYING MOTIVATED

Moms are amazing creatures. You'd think we should own a hat store; we wear so many of them. But every now and then we run into a rut. It's hard work staying motivated, upbeat, and optimistic. That's why it's critical to have mood boosters, the things you can rely on to motivate you when your drive has slipped into neutral.

## MomsTown Tips
### TO CONTINUE YOUR MOMENTUM

- When you feel stuck, start writing.
- Go back to the beginning of your thirty-day process and repeat.
- Get some exercise.
- Drink another bottle of water.
- Breathe.
- Talk to your buddy, mentors, and those who support you.
- And heck, if you're really stuck, go shopping for a new handbag or a great pair of shoes! Nothing like a little more debt to keep you motivated!

## Daily Strategizing Tips

MomsTown works on a daily timeline. That means we work every day. Every day we brainstorm, and almost daily we do something uncomfortable, such as make a cold call. We want you to do something uncomfortable every day.

- If you have a buddy you work with, have brainstorming sessions. *Every day!*
- Write down your strategy for getting your business off the ground and for attracting clients. Come up with a new idea every day.
- Realize that every day is different. Learn to roll with the

punches when your plan for the day is altered owing to family or other responsibilities.

⊙ The key is in doing something—*every day*, no matter what the distractions may be.

---

When I thought I couldn't go on, I forced myself to keep going. My success is based on persistence, not luck.

—*Norman Lear*

---

# A FEW NOT-SO-FINAL WORDS

Congratulations! The Unique You is on your way to MomsTown Big Break success. Be proud of your accomplishments. Know that success comes in small doses and big payoffs, and always be ready for a surprise.

This is a good time to take a deep breath and get ready to build on the solid foundation you've set in place. Starting and growing a business is an exciting yet challenging endeavor.

It is not for the faint of heart. You will work long hours, experience setbacks and letdowns: that's the reality. However, believing in your crazy dream, developing a successful strategy, and executing your plan are the beginning steps of a promising and profitable future. Go for it! E-mail us at bigbreak@momstown.com and tell us how you're doing. We wish you great success and fun along the way. We believe in you.

## Resources

Small Business Administration, www.sba.gov

U.S. Patent and Trademark Office, www.uspto.gov

Small Business Success, www.smallbusinesssuccess.com

MicroEnterprise Journal, www.microenterprisejournal.com

Money Magazine, www.moneymagazine.com

Business Women's Network, www.bwni.com

Small Business & Self-Employed One-Stop Resource,
    www.Apps.irs.gov/businesses/small/index.html

SBA's Women's Business Center, www.onlinewbc.com

www.bizwomen.com

American Business Women's Association, www.abwahq.org

Business Plan Services, www.windhaus.com

Forum for Women Entrepreneurs, www.fwe.org

*Chapter 14*

# Evolving into the Unique You

$\mathcal{I}$f you are just learning about MomsTown and our incredible network of women, we would like to welcome you. It has always been our mission to support women with words of encouragement and inspiration, and to follow up with practical tips, resources, and information you can use.

We know your time is valuable, your energy is treasured, and your thoughts cherished. It means the world to us that you are joining us on a journey of renewal, a journey to discover the Unique You. In this book we have looked at many aspects of women's busy lives. We don't doubt that there are facets of your life that we may have overlooked. We have tried our best to be the conduit between the amazing community of MomsTown moms, experts we have interviewed, and you. We are genuinely excited about the future and the positive changes you're about to make.

That's the good news.

The bad news (or shall we say, "the challenging news") is that you have now joined us in leaving the comfort zone and are now facing a possibly unfamiliar world of new possibilities. It's scary to have this much freedom. It's scary to realize that you have begun a journey of evolution that will take you to unknown heights and experiences. It's scary to realize that you may try things you have never thought of trying before, that you will reach out beyond what you thought you could do. And yes, you will face some failures, because that is part of the learning, evolutionary process. But they will be *your* failures: goals you reached for and couldn't quite grasp—until next time.

We recognize change doesn't always come easily. It's most often easier to just stay the course, especially when things seem to be going okay. But is that what you really want: an okay life? Or do you want and deserve better? Of course *you want better.* Even when life is good, improvements can be made; stronger friendships can be built; more determination can be instilled; you can continue your work raising great kids; you can have better sex, make more money, and become fitter and healthier. There are always new things to learn, new experiences to have, and new paths to explore.

Let's also be clear about one more thing: all this effort to have more free time, be more organized, make more money, and feel better about yourself is not intended to make you a better Stepford Wife.

**The point of the Unique You is to empower you to make your own conscious and deliberate choices about your future.**

Women who get out from under the laundry pile may not be able to "have it all." But they sure as heck can have more than they have at present. If we have simply taught you how to be the perfect mother to your children and a great sex machine for your husband without seeing the rich potential within yourself as a woman—within each of us as women—then we have failed.

> Do not go where the path may lead, go instead
> where there is no path and leave a trail.
> —*Ralph Waldo Emerson*

When you're exploring, it's fun to venture off the beaten path and go where you haven't gone before. New trails can be exciting, but when you become a mother, they can also become scary; you become cautious and apprehensive. You worry about potential outcomes. You worry about the downside.

> *All of a sudden I've become Safety Woman. I worry about the safety of my kids and my husband, and I worry about my own safety way more than when I was single. It has even changed the way I ski. I used to be a daredevil, willing to tackle the black diamond runs. Now I stick to the intermediate runs, afraid of breaking a leg or something worse. —Sue*

We understand this change in Sue because it's the same change we experienced when we became moms. It's only natural that moms evolve into more cautious women. We have a lot of responsibilities, and a lot of people depend on us. But we also have a lot of people looking to us to set an example. We want our children to approach life with gusto, to be willing to take risks (nothing life-threatening, of course), and to live life as the great adventure that it can be.

## READY FOR THE UNIQUE YOU? IT'S YOUR CHOICE

To be a bold woman takes bold moves. We know we are getting smarter and stronger as we get older, so why is it sometimes we don't feel or act on that sense? We allow our lives to become about everyone else, and we lose who we are in the process. We love our kids, we love our husbands (or we love that they're no longer our husbands), and for the most part, we love our lives.

But at this very moment we want you to make a choice. Choose to focus on the Unique You. Think about your dreams, your passions, what's important to you, and what you want to do with your life. It is possible to be a wife, a mother, and a vibrant woman, and it's never too late. We know this because we read e-mails and forum posts from thousands of women just like us, and we talk to them on the radio. All over America, women are reinventing themselves and loving it.

As the first step toward the Unique You, take a fresh look at the choices you make on a daily basis that have an impact on the kind of lifestyle you want to live. The acronym CHOICE helps illustrate how one word can be a step toward profound change.

**C**ategorize
**H**ome in
**O**wn
**I**nitiate
**C**reate
**E**xecute

What does CHOICE really mean when you take it apart? Here's what it means to us:

**Categorize.** Consider the many compartments of your life: children at home, children at school, meals, money, time, romance/sex, girlfriends, lookin' good, or personal meditation—just for starters. What are you doing now in each category and how can you do it better? We have given you some tips in these areas; we will have tons more as moms all over the country continue to contribute ideas and suggestions. Take a swing at setting up the categories that fit your life: it's one good way to evaluate your starting point.

**Home in.** Are there subcategories of the ideas you have selected? Can you home in on specific repetitive tasks, problems, solutions, or ideas in each category? Can you refine the challenges you identify in terms of the Unique You?

**Own.** See these categories in personal terms. After all, this is your life—the starting point for the Unique You. Don't be afraid to express your feelings about each one of these categories and subcategories you have defined. The more you own the issues and the challenges, the more you are taking hold of your own life.

**Initiate.** Take matters into your own hands—one step at a time. Being proactive about every aspect of your life will make you more aware and sensitive to the potential of the Unique You. Try some of the ideas that have been suggested in the chapters of this book. Talk with your girlfriends and learn what works for them. Then those challenges that you have made personal and specific can be met with personal and specific solutions.

**Create.** As we admitted at the outset, we're not geniuses, we don't have all the answers—for ourselves or for you. But we have created a new future for ourselves, and we are helping other moms to do the same. You can do it too. Creating isn't just for Michelangelo. It's for everyone, and it can be fun and exciting. Be creative in your approach to solving problems in those categories and creative in finding a Unique You.

**Execute.** Oh, yeah. You've got to do stuff. If you do stuff, more stuff happens, usually good stuff. This is the final part of CHOICE, the part where you put your ideas into action. It's not good if you think you've figured out some answers but are afraid to act on them. This part takes courage. It can be the most thrilling and the most nerve-wracking part of the process. However, the more you do it, the easier it becomes. And the Unique You will emerge.

\* \* \*

There is one final point we'd like to make on the subject of choice; if you don't make choices for yourself, others will make them for you.

Your husband, your mother, your children—they'll all be too happy to tell you what to do with newfound time and energy.

We know that it's impossible for anyone to give you a list of priorities in the pursuit of your dreams, but it is possible to allow others to inspire you. We invite you to MomsTown to find inspiration and to inspire others. Know that it is a legitimate endeavor to redefine yourself. In fact, it is a "real job" to set aside the time and take yourself seriously. Also know that you might have to sell other people on your quest; when you do, it will be worth it. To gain the support of your family and perhaps reach out (networking again) to kindred spirits will help to keep you motivated.

It may be tough to begin, but we'll support you, and so will all the other moms in MomsTown. You are not alone. In fact, you've just joined a pretty nifty club. We're evolving. We're constantly reinventing ourselves, and you can reinvent yourself too. It's fun. It opens new doors and new potential.

On this path, you may discover that you are impeded by your own fears. Katharine Hepburn told all of us, "Face your dragons." Cut them into small pieces and put names on them:

- Husband will be upset.
- Children will feel abandoned.
- I'm too old for change.
- I'm afraid of failure.
- This is selfish.
- There's never enough time.
- Do I dare to dream so boldly?

Then recognize that many of these fears are small, imaginary, or surmountable. Don't allow such impediments to stand in the way of your new life. Be brave.

\* \* \*

It's now time to look forward to the Unique You.

The Unique You isn't going to rest on her laurels. The Unique You is gathering energy and momentum. We all have the potential to lead a better life, a more enriching life that inspires us and everyone who comes into contact with us, especially our husbands, kids, family, and friends.

Now it's time for you to make a promise to yourself. When you put down this book, we want you to do these ten things:

1. Take five deep breaths—in through the nose and out through the mouth. Five slow breaths might sound like a lot, but we want you to truly relax and feel the cleansing of deep breathing.

2. Write down one change you want to make immediately, just one. It can be a physical, mental, or environmental change. It doesn't matter if it's big or small: the key is to start with just one.

3. Tell one person, a friend or family member, the change you want to make.

4. Do one thing to initiate the change. Perhaps you need to schedule an appointment, come up with a plan to clean out a closet, or set your alarm clock ahead by thirty minutes to get in a brisk morning walk.

5. Congratulate yourself on completing the one task, and then tell a friend or family member about your accomplishment. Accept their praise.

6. Determine the next step you need to take—and take it.

7. Try to be consistent with the same change each day for the next twenty-one days. Experts say that it takes three weeks for a change to become a habit.

8. Once you've established the first Unique You habit, declare another change you want to make.

9. Repeat the cycle.

10. Enjoy the thrill of learning and empowering yourself.

You are on the road to becoming all you want to be. You take the first step when you admit to yourself that you have great potential. Start today by surrounding yourself with positive images, positive people, and rekindled optimism. You create. You are a woman. All of the courage, determination, confidence, and enthusiasm you need is within you; tap into it. If you need support, whether it's occasional support or daily support, we are all here for you. We've said it before, and we'll say it again: MomsTown moms are supportive, smart, and always ready to help.

The Unique You is arriving. Welcome her with open arms. Be kind to her. Let her try new things with the understanding that they won't always work out. Be willing to let her fail. In failure we often find our greatest success. The Unique You will change your life in ways you can't even imagine at this moment. Just as your children changed your life in ways you could have never predicted, the Unique You is about to deliver some unexpected surprises. Savor every moment.

# ACKNOWLEDGMENTS

**Mary's Acknowledgments:**

I am so grateful for the support and belief from my family. I am lucky to be married to a loving husband who is my steadfast supporter. Thank you, Bill, for seeing my potential and believing in me, I love you. Sterling and Portia, my sweet daughters, you both are the inspiration and driving force behind everything I do. Thanks to my mom, and brothers and sisters. Special thanks to my sister Pam for always believing in me, my brother Peter for your unending support, and to my sister-in-law, Diana, and Gideon. To Margaret Rendler, a very special mother-in-law, and to the rest of the Rendler family, thank you.

Thanks to my friends Allison Maslan, for being an example of what a true and best girlfriend is; Robert and Stacie Luly, you are great friends and I appreciate you so much; Chris and Jane Flanders, thank you for loving me as your friend unconditionally; Anne and Steve Eyl, thank you for your friendship; Erin Begley, you have been a great help with the children while I worked; Karen Stowe, you are a great golfing buddy; Jason Waiton, for being a good friend and the best fitness trainer I know.

Writing this book has been an eye-opening and cathartic experience. I've learned how to be a better wife, mother, and friend. I've learned that I have the power of choice: the power to choose my attitude, my outlook, and my actions. That power is liberating and I've become more enthusiastic about the possibilities for me and my family.

**Heather's Acknowledgments:**

I am blessed to be loved and to have the support of so many. I am grateful to be married to one of the good guys. Thank you, Steve, for loving me so completely and for being so easy to love. Thank you for all of your support. I want to thank the other three loves of my life, Evan, Hayden, and Nolan. You make my life whole. Thank you for teaching me, loving me, and inspiring me every day to be and do better. I am so proud of each of you for the kindness, love, and joy you bring to all of us.

Thank you to my parents, Beverly and Charles Jennings. You both have truly been there since the beginning and that means the world. It is with your love and nurturing that I feel confident that I am a good woman and a good mom. To my sister Paige Jennings, you are an amazing source of inspiration. I am so proud to be your sister. To my Grandma, Nellie Askegreen, thank you for holding my hand every time you kiss me. To my Grandma Mary Jennings who passed away during the writing of this book, rest in peace and love with Grandpa.

To the rest of my family, lots of hugs and kisses, as always. To my parents-in-law, Ken and Judy Reider, thank you for loving us so completely. To Mike, Brian, Teresa, Quinncie, Meghann, and Blake, my love and we'll see you at the river.

To the two best girlfriends a woman could wish for, Kim Kinahan and Laura van Dam, I love you both, I'm thrilled to continue growing up with the two of you. To Cecilia and Cap Haiger, thank you for all the family play dates. To Dana and Joe Mares, cheers to all of the date nights.

## From the Two of Us

First and foremost, we would like to thank all the women who make MomsTown a thriving community. We appreciate your e-mails, calls in to our radio show, and posts on our MomsTown forum. You are the reason this book exists. This book truly is *all about you*. We are inspired by your passion for family and your creative ideas. We are honored to have you a part of our world.

Terry Wood and Kathy Samuels, thank you for welcoming us into the CBS/Paramount family and for teaching us the ropes. We are grateful to be working with you and for your guidance and help in managing and developing our brand.

Dr. Phil, thank you for your advice, guidance, time, and thoughtfulness. Thank you for helping us to connect the dots and the importance of taking action every day. You have been instrumental in the shaping and success of this book and we are fortunate to have your coaching and mentorship. We also appreciate you for introducing us to Jan Miller of Dupree/Miller and Associates so this book could come to fruition.

Thank you Carla Pennington, Kandi Amelon-Sawyer, Jill Skinner, and the rest of the Dr. Phil team.

Robin, we know there's always a good woman next to a good man. Thank you for being so kind and for being a great role model.

To Jan Miller, our literary agent, our deepest gratitude for helping us put this book together. Thanks also for a whirlwind day in New York City. We wish everyone could experience New York with Jan Miller. And to our team at Dupree/Miller; to Shannon Miser-Marven, thank you for your dedication and hard work behind the scenes. Nena Madonia, thank you for your enthusiasm and for always keeping this project on track. Annabelle Baxter, and the rest of the team, thank you for all that you do.

A huge thank you to our editor, Dominick Anfuso, at Free Press for believing in our message. We instantly felt embraced and welcomed. Your sincerity, kindness, and direction are appreciated more than you can imagine. To Maria Bruk Aupérin, thank you for your diligence, belief in our message, and for fine-tuning the manuscript. You truly are a pro. To Carisa Hays, Jill Siegel, and Suzanne Donahue, thank you for your enthusiasm for this book and for getting the word out.

David Boxerbaum, our talent agent, thank you for seeing what we believe in and for always being there for us. And we still agree with you that MomsTown is definitely a sitcom. This is all happening because of you. Melissa Orton, thanks to you for handling all of the details.

Joe Ferullo, thank you for helping us visualize other brand opportunities and for being an all around nice guy.

To our legal eagles, Joe Lesko, Eric Suddelson, and Clark Siegel. Joe, thank you for believing in MomsTown since the idea was first conceived, for your guidance, and for not charging us for all of your great advice, you are a good friend. Eric and Clark, thank you for making legal rounds in Hollywood a piece of cake.

Speaking of good guys, a special thanks to Reid Tracy at Hay House. Thank you for giving us a radio home and for truly helping guide this ship. We'd also like to thank Summer McStravick, Sonny Salinas, Roberto Criado, Joe Bartlett, Kyle Rector, and Diane Ray.

To our business mentor, friend, and great guy, Mark LeBlanc, thank you for turning the Rubik's Cube with us and helping us develop our laser-like focus.

Kelly Poelker, thanks for keeping everything running smoothly and picking up the loose ends. You are our favorite virtual assistant.

To the many experts who shared their wisdom and advice within the pages of this book: Dr. Michael Roizen, Dr. Laura Berman, Dr. Scott Miller, Terah Kathryn Collins, Julie Morgenstern, Eddie Osterland.

Last but not least, to Digby Diehl (aka, Charlie). What can we say? With your savoir faire this book hit the mark and you've taught us how to be better writers. You are the real deal and we're lucky to now have you as a real friend. To Kay Diehl and Catherine, we appreciate your behind-the-scenes research and editing. We thank you.

One final thanks to the staff at Meritage for providing us with the corner table, a chilled glass, and fine food. You helped to keep the creative juices flowing.

# ABOUT THE AUTHORS

MARY GOULET began her career on Wall Street as an institutional bond salesperson. After nine successful years, she moved to California and opened a real estate company. She also sang professionally and became a licensed holistic health practitioner. Since June of 2002, Mary has hosted two shows under the *Entrepreneur* magazine brand. She also cohosted a local show for the *Union-Tribune San Diego's* online edition, SignOnSanDiego.com. Mary resides in San Diego with her husband and two daughters.

HEATHER REIDER graduated from San Diego State University in 1989 with a degree in journalism. She enjoyed a ten-year career on air as a television news reporter and anchor, working for CBS, NBC, and ABC affiliates on the West Coast. She covered historical events for CBS, including a live interview aboard Air Force One with Bill Clinton. Heather resides in San Diego with her husband and three boys.